A BACKWARD GLANCE

A BACKWARD GLANCE

Eileen Briggs

The Book Guild Ltd
Sussex, England

The Book Guild Ltd.
25 High Street,
Lewes, Sussex

First published 1998
© Eileen Briggs 1998

Set in Times
Typesetting by
Acorn Bookwork, Salisbury, Wiltshire

Printed in Great Britain by
Bookcraft (Bath) Ltd. Avon

A catalogue record for this book is
available from the British Library

ISBN 1 85776 259 2

This book is dedicated to the memory of Edith Drew, school teacher for many years through my childhood at Bullbrook School, Bracknell, Berkshire.

CONTENTS

ACKNOWLEDGEMENTS

Thank you to all local friends and relatives who have shared their stories and reminiscences with me.

Mrs P. Buddery, The late Miss M. Buxton, The late Mr Arthur Briggs, Adelaide, Australia. Mr G. Butcher, Mrs M. Cheney, The late Mr A. Cole, Mrs D. Edwards, Mrs Ewing. The late Mrs M. Gale, Mrs E. Hope, Mrs P. Keat, The late Mrs W. Langley, and the late Mr L. Langley, Miss Alice Matthews, Mrs H. Mann, Mrs K. Morris and the late Mr E. Morris, Mr R. Morris, Mrs J. Napper, The late Mrs Norris, Mrs J. Randle and Mrs Welsh. Mr Frank James, Australia.

Photographs and Illustrations

Photographs by Mr Yorke, kindly lent by the late Mrs M. Hutson.
Mr Kenneth Hope's kindly lent by his widow Mrs Eileen Hope.
Mr A. Briggs, Miss M. Buxton, Mrs D. Edwards, Mrs M. Briggs, Mrs P. Harvey, Mrs K. Morris and the late Mr E. Morris, Mr R. Morris, the late Mrs M. Gale, Mrs W. Langley, Mrs P. Keat.
Alexander Pope, Percy Shelley, (*Childrens Encyclopedia* edited by Arthur Mee.)
Charles Kinsley (*Childrens Encyclopedia* edited by Arthur Mee)
Oscar Wilde, by Napoleon Sarony 1882. (Library of Congress.)

Scrapbook Picture Cuttings

Wokingham & Bracknell Gazette, Bracknell News, Bracknell & Wokingham Times.
Reading Mercury, Bracknell News Extra.

INTRODUCTION

When my father spent the princely sum of 18 shillings on a book of
Berkshire and settled down in his fireside chair for a quiet read, I still
remember his great disappointment on finding that Bracknell was
mentioned in only a couple of short sentences, one of which says,
'One of the best stretches of road in the County takes us to Bracknell,
and unless it is market day, we would be best to push on through to
Ascot, there is little of beauty to be seen.' Unfortunately, another
famous author and television personality gave an equally unflattering
description of our little market town, and needless to say, as a Brack-
nellian who was happily living and working in this friendly village, I
have always wanted to put the record straight and say something in
Bracknell's favour. But alas I am not an author but just an ordinary
housewife and observer of what goes on in and around in my home
town.

As it was around the time when rumours started circulating that
Bracknell was one of the areas chosen for the development of a New
Town, I have often wondered if the ill-timed views and comments of
these two eminent gentlemen on their hasty visits through Bracknell,
and their equally hasty judgements of our area afterwards, maybe
helped towards sealing our future fate by giving a totally untrue
picture that Bracknell had nothing that was worthy of saving. Sadly,
in the coming years the village of our grandparents rapidly disappeared in the almost total destruction of the little old market town
that we loved so dearly. In fact, it became the village that disappeared.
The relief felt in escaping Hitler's attention was to be short-lived, as
the future architects of Bracknell were to achieve more destruction in
the coming years than the villagers could have imagined. What made
it worse were the letters full of promise that their homes and shops
would be safe from development.

I think that we owe it to the past and the future generations of
Bracknellians to leave a more fitting picture of Bracknell than two
short sentences saying there was little of beauty to be seen. Our
children and grandchildren need to be able to read more of the past
life in this area when this present generation has itself passed on.

Eighteen shillings was quite a large amount to pay out of the wages
that Father received, and this book was considered a little luxury item
on his part. He spent a great deal of time reading after a hard day's

work. Little did Father realise as he sat in his armchair that the very room he was sitting in would shortly be demolished by the bulldozers.

As he sat there, I think that he was hoping to read something about Bracknell's Old High Street, with its quaint jumble of characteristic little stores where one could find any item that was desired. Not for us the journey into Reading or London for those special little things that seem no longer available here in the modern age. Each shop was filled to overflowing with every conceivable item imaginable. So crammed with stock were they that they looked positively untidy by today's standards, but oh, so inviting. To go into the dark and mysterious inner sanctums of these little shops was like going into Aladdin's cave. But the storekeepers always knew exactly where to find each item, and the reply 'It is out of stock' was practically unheard of then.

Gone now too is Church Road, where the cattle were driven along every market day, to and from the station, and anyone silly enough to leave their garden gate open on a Thursday would return home to find the odd sheep or cow being rounded up by the herdsmen. We once had a long convoy of cows trundle up our garden path, each one peering in at us sitting at the table, as they sauntered past the window. Mother opened the door about an inch, saying 'Shoo, shoo', which didn't do a lot of good; they quietly ambled on around the garden at their leisure as if she wasn't there. But the farmer soon located his lost animals and marched them back out again, each one casually staring in at us having our tea. Cows have such big, sorrowful, brown eyes. Gone too are the green fields all around, where they used to peacefully graze.

Although Bracknell was a thriving market town, life was spent at a more leisurely pace in those days. Shopping was a pleasure and one chatted away happily to the shopkeepers about the latest news and happenings around the village. There was none of the rush of today's supermarkets, where if you do not pack your goods quickly enough off the conveyor belt, you are aware of a long queue of disgruntled faces. People are programmed, rather like a row of automated soldiers, to march through the checkouts in the fastest time possible; but in fact it can take anything up to 15 minutes on a busy day.

BRACKNELL

We lived in a village, it being quite small,
If we walked down the street, we were known by all.
Cheerfully greeting, as we went on our way,
The doctor, the grocer, the children at play.

Our house wasn't large, just three up and three down,
Preferred by us all to life in a town.
A home full of memories, and such loving care,
Happy our lives, with neighbours to share.

In the woods that were scattered, all around,
Violets and bluebells grew thick on the ground.
Small tinkling streams, and silent still pools,
Where tired little feet were dangled to cool

Where the author's family home used to be, in Victoria Road

1

Market days were Thursdays, where children stood charmed,
By chickens and animals brought down from the farms.
When young ones were married, the villagers would cheer,
To make them the happiest occasions of the year.

When out of the blue, some strangers one day,
Came with some plans to take our village away.
Fight as we might, we just could not delay
The bulldozers from sweeping our house right away.

As year follows year, more concrete we see,
Now there's a car park, where our home used to be.
The pools are filled in, our streams underground,
Nothing but office blocks, not a violet can be found.

Architects come, and architects go,
Leaving their monstrosities, all on show.
Where do they live? Oh no, no, not here,
Where even the badgers have to live in fear.

A BACKWARD GLANCE AT BRITAIN'S PREHISTORY

Some 4,000 million years ago, the hot molten mass which was then our earth began to crust over so that by the Ordovician period of 500 million years ago, the Britain that we know today began to appear with the foundations of sandstones and muds, which later became shales, trapping early fossils of that period.

300 million years ago came the Carboniferous Age, of swamps and wonderful tropical forests, which were to eventually form the coal seams of Britain.

250 million years ago, the land had turned into arid hot deserts, with windblown sandstorms. Dominating the landscape were the deltaic flats.

170 million years ago, the seascape included sharks, reptilian ichthyosaurs, and bat-winged pterosaurs. The scarped nature of the Cotswolds was formed in this period.

100 million years ago came the Cretaceous period, with a subtropical landscape, and large reptiles roaming the land. The Alpine movement formed the chalk Downs, after the land had previously been blanketed in chalk mud, which later consolidated over millions of years.

Man appeared towards the end of the million years of the Pleistocene period. This interglacial time was marked by successive advances and retreats of the polar ice, thus developing the landscape of Britain as we know it today. The earliest human fossil remains found in Britain were Swanscombe Man, dating from the late Hoxnian Interglacial period of about 250,000 years ago.

200,000 years ago, when north of the Thames was covered in ice, the large woolly mammoth roamed around our countryside. Around 10,000 years ago the temperatures began to rise.

Man lived in small groups for thousands of years, making little impact on the environment. Later, with their rough stone tools, their advancement began to gain pace. Also the keeping of domestic animals began a reshaping of nature, by stopping forest regeneration and fostering the grassland development.

The Neolithic Age brought migrants from the Mediterranean. Previously the Mesolithic men used to roam from place to place in their search for food. Farming was to put an end to this gathering way of life.

3

The Neolithic people built impressive earthworks, which can still be seen today, many of these being in Wiltshire. Around 4,000 years ago they were the first people to permanently alter their natural surroundings.

Some authors date Herne the Hunter right back to Palaeolithic Man. In *The God of Witches*, Margaret Murray writes of '...the figure ... of a man clothed in the skin of a stag, and wearing antlers on his head.' She dates this as Palaeolithic. Others date Herne to the Middle Ages as Master of Cain's Pack.

The formation of the Channel and the North Sea had begun by 6,500 BC. Long barrows ceased around 2,500 BC.

Early Neolithic people started mining for flint and other rocks, and once farming was established, this allowed them time for other pursuits such as making polished axes for their earthwork buildings. The first part of Stonehenge and the Aubrey Holes date from the Neolithic period. Enormous effort was put in, over several centuries, for this henge monument; its meaning is still very obscure.

The Beaker people came over to Britain from the Continent, and the Bronze Age began. Interments favoured round mounds, instead of the long barrows of previous peoples. From 2,000 BC round barrows became the major funerary rite. Round barrows can be found in Bracknell and Easthampstead.

1,000 BC, little groups of roundhouses, with ditch and bank enclosed farmyards, would have been a feature of our local landscape around this time, when mixed farming was practised. Local ponds and streams supplied the water needed.

From the seventh century BC the introduction of iron working began in Britain. Agricultural changes, with settlement patterns gradually developing from those of the last of the Bronze Age. Ranch boundaries were used in the control of animals, and crops of wheat and barley were now grown, also the Celtic bean.

With the coming of the Iron Age, from the late Bronze Age, Hillforts appeared. A fine example of one of these, can be found on the Nine Mile Ride, now known as Caesar's Camp. To say that Bracknell has no history, is ridiculous, as evidence of early settlements, are all around us.

Celtic graves were often lavishly furnished. The most outstanding were the graves of the warriors, containing chariots. The Celtic Druidic priesthood placated spirits, with rituals that were considered barbaric by the Romans, which seems strange when one considers what went on in the Rome Colosseum, particularly the practice of throwing people to the lions.

4

BRITAIN'S HISTORY

The arrival of the Romans to our shores, marked the end of prehistory, and the beginning of recorded history. The British language also changed to a Germanic dialect.

In AD 43 Britain became a Roman province. Although the Iron Age hill forts were like small towns, they were very little in comparison to the Roman towns which were to follow: Londinium (London); Camulodunum (Colchester); Verulamium (St Albans); Calleva (Silchester); Durovernum (Canterbury); Aquae Sulis (Bath); Glevum (Gloucester); Deva (Chester); Lindum (Lincoln); Eburacum (York). The Londinium (London) to Calleva (Silchester) road passed close by the area on which Bracknell now stands. Ramblers still walk along the route of part of this Roman road (The Devil's Highway).

Before the Romans, Britain had very unco-ordinated settlements with little or no communication between each. The Romans and their road building provided the first links between towns throughout the country.

With the withdrawal of the Romans came the Dark Ages, which lasted 600 years. Ireland was converted to Christianity by Roman missionaries, from there the Irish monks spread the Christian message to Anglo-Saxons and Picts in Britain. The Anglo-Saxons arrived in the fifth and sixth centuries, coming to Britain from Germany and Scandinavia. By the end of the seventh century there were three large kingdoms in England: Wessex in the south, Mercia in the midlands, and Northumbria in the north and southern Scotland. Wales was never conquered.

During the ninth century a second invasion of Vikings settled in eastern England, then gradually pushed their way westwards inland. Many Viking weapons have been recovered from the Thames. The Danish King Cnut reigned from 1016 to 1035, Edward the Confessor came to the throne in 1042.

The Norman Conquest in 1066 unified England once more, and slavery was abolished by the Normans. Norman castles began to appear in ever increasing numbers. The castle at Windsor was first made of wood, but soon progressed to the great stone keeps that we know today.

SOME DATES AND LOCAL HISTORY OF OUR NEIGHBOURHOODS

The *Domesday Book* records that Easthampstead belonged to Westminster Abbey. Half of Easthampstead was uninhabited, as its lands were set aside for royal hunting.

By 1184 Windsor Castle was already a massive structure of thick walls, built of immensely large slabs of heathstone. The Saxon kings had all hunted locally. William I taught his sons hunting, who later became William II, and Henry I, who in 1110 held court at New Windsor.

Henry II became king in 1154, his queen was Eleanor of Aquitaine. Henry was short and fat, and a little mad. His table manners were appalling. His straggling royal caravan must have been a familiar sight, rumbling over local rough roads to the hunting lodges hereabouts.

The Plantagenet kings had a hunting lodge at Easthampstead, as many orders were issued from there. In later years a message was sent on 12 January 1321, to the sheriffs to catch a lunatic called Robert Lewer, who was frightening the King's subjects. In 1215 the Great Charter was signed at Runnymede by King John. Throughout the reign of Henry III Windsor Castle was growing and changing.

During the reigns of Edward I and II in 1272 to 1327, hunting was carried out in Ashridge Wood, Wokingham, and the Earl of Lincoln was refused permission to cultivate 100 acres, as it was against the King's interest to do so. A Market Charter was passed in 1219, for a market to be held in Wokingham on Tuesdays. The reign of Edward III saw the beginning of the Hundred Years War against France in 1337.

A temporary court was set up in Wokingham in 1333 to try some men who were behind with their rent payments, but the session ended in uproar when the circuit judges were attacked by the men, so they dared not to proceed. The Black Death almost halved the population in 1348–9. In 1350 King Edward III built a hunting lodge in Easthampstead. After this time many future kings and queens of England were to visit Easthampstead for the sport of hunting. In 1381 Richard II used Easthampstead as a hunting box.

In Dorchester Abbey can be found a Wokingham bell donated before 1383, a product of the Wokingham bell foundry. A Dorchester

Abbey model is in the hand of Saint Birinus, in the South transept window of Holy Trinity, Bracknell. Saint Birinus brought Christianity to the Thames Valley in 634. In the year 1434, Henry VI was staying at Easthampstead. By the end of this century, the Wokingham bell foundry was moved to Reading.

1528 found King Henry VIII in Easthampstead Park 'in search of greater game', while in 1531, poor Queen Catherine of Aragon was receiving messengers from the King, pressing her for a divorce. 1539 saw the Dissolution of the Monasteries. The monastery at Hurley was already destroyed in 1535.

1538 saw the trial of Lord Montague of Okyngham. Although loyal to Henry VIII, Lord Montague was deeply upset over the Dissolution of the Monasteries. He was found guilty of treason, and was executed on Tower Hill along with the Marquess of Exeter.

Henry VIII loved his hunting around the local woodlands so much that some days he would hunt from nine in the morning until the evening. There are not any accounts of visits to Easthampstead by Edward VI, Henry VIII's son, who was probably too delicate to hunt in the saddle all day. Mary I, his sister, does not appear to have come hunting either, but carried out a wholesale massacre of Protestants, and re-established the monasteries her father had dissolved. But Elizabeth I spent many happy hours hunting locally, and also took of the waters of Gorrick Well, which was well known for its healing properties. There were many plots against Queen Elizabeth I; the biggest threat came from Spain with the Armada. Preparations against the armada included Warfield churchwardens' accounts for a constable to watch the beacon and for firewood. A bell foundry was established in 1560 by Thomas Eldridge in Wokingham.

In 1622–3, James I resided at Easthampstead in the summer months. In 1625 came the accession of Charles I, who wanted absolute power, while the House pressed for the sovereignty of Parliament. The result of this clash was that the King ruled for 11 years without a Parliament; during this period of personal government, he was helped by Archbishop Laud, who was born in Reading, but whose parents previously lived in Wokingham. Archbishop Laud was executed in 1645, after the Civil War started in 1642. After the execution of Charles I, England was governed for 11 years by Oliver Cromwell and his army.

Meanwhile, back in 1628 Easthampstead Park had been granted to William Trumbull for his services to Archduke Albert of Austria in the Netherlands. Trumbull was to provide 200 deer for the King's recreation. Later the Trumbulls were released from this obligation by Charles II.

During this century there was the danger of infection from the plague in London. The plague, which visited London with such terrible consequences, was followed by the great fire of London, which destroyed most of the squalid slums which were responsible for the rapid spread of the plague.

Charles II spent a lot of time during this period at Windsor Castle, enjoying the company of Nell Gwynne, the charming orange vendor. Their natural son the Duke of St Albans was later in life made Lord Lieutenant of Berkshire.

James II was on the throne for only three years, before being replaced by his two daughters of his first wife, Anne Hyde: Mary, born in 1662, and Anne, born in 1665. Mary's husband William was not well liked due to a streak of brutality which he showed at the massacre of Glencoe. Mary died of Smallpox in 1694, her husband in 1702.

Back in 1670, the highwayman Claud Duval was hanged at Tyburn. He was reputed to have a hideout in Wokingham. Dick Turpin occasionally operated locally; his reputed hideout was in Bracknell.

In 1685, many Huguenots were driven out of France into England. At the end of this century the father of Alexander Pope moved his family to live in Binfield. Alexander was encouraged by Sir William Trumbull to write *Pastorals* which were published in 1704–6.

Queen Anne was the originator of Royal Ascot in 1711. The first race was run on 11 August. It was advertised that Her Majesty's Plate of 100 guineas would be run round the new heat on Ascot Common near Windsor. Queen Anne and her husband were fond of hunting; when she became old and gouty, she laid out drives for her use in a chaise with one horse.

In 1716 the Pope family left Binfield. Popes Meadow is named after the poet. 1727 was the year in which the ballad of 'Molly Mogg', was published. Molly was the daughter of the landlord of the Rose Inn, which was then situated next to the Bush.

1745 saw the Jacobite Uprising, with the young pretender, Bonnie Prince Charlie. The 1759 Turnpike Act provided for a new turnpike road from Virginia Water through to New Bracknowl and Wokingham to Old Gallows. 1781, George III completed rides through forest for hunting. A stag got away after a five hour hunt. 1786, Mary, the granddaughter of William Trumbull IV, married Arthur Hill, who became the 2nd Marquess of Downshire.

Smallpox was still taking its toll on the local population. The Warfield Overseer's account book reads, 'May 18th 1794 to Widow Littlewood in smallpox £1 12s 0d. May 26th 1794 to burying Widow Littlewood. £1 14s 3d. In 1801 there is an entry of 'To Mr Reeves bill for Inoculation', seven years after the widow had died from smallpox.

1807–12, the building of The Royal Military Academy at Sandhurst was completed. 1813, the savage forest laws were repealed by an act of enclosure of Windsor Forest. Conifer plantations are started, and the forest ceased to exist in its old form. The Duke of Wellington regularly stayed at the Rose Inn, on his way to Stratfield Saye.

1821, bull-baiting was prohibited in Wokingham and Bracknell. Bulls were still provided as meat for the poor on Christmas Day.

1830, formation of a Forest Association for the protection of farms from incendiarists setting fire to barns and haystacks by labourers who disliked the introduction of new agricultural machinery. A motion was proposed by the Marquess of Downshire and seconded by Robert Palmer, Esq., MP. Each parish was to have its own police force of special constables to apprehend the incendiarists.

1833, the last bull-baiting in England. An Act of Parliament banned this cruel sport.

1843, there was an affray at Ascot between some privates of the 45th Regiment, then quartered at Windsor, and hordes of thimblerig- gers and other thieves who were gathered there. The thieves got the worst of it. Several soldiers had been robbed during the day, but the police had kept any fights under control. Later in the evening, however, just after seven o'clock, a quarrel took place between a private and a gypsy. The gypsy, who was the aggressor, got a deserved thrashing, but this was the signal for 300 or 400 keepers of thimblerig-tables and gipsies to join in. The redcoats came off the victors, but not before several men had fractured limbs on both sides.

1845, Queen Victoria halted at the Red Lion in Bracknell, and was given a rousing reception by the inhabitants. The next stop was in Wokingham, before going on to Stratfield Saye to visit the Duke of Wellington.

1847, Richard Miliard at this time held the Hinds Head. The village of Bracknell consisted of a long narrow street, inhabited principally by small shopkeepers. The Crown Inn was first listed around this time, and was situated where the post office now stands. The roads were said to be remarkably good around Bracknell.

1853, South Hill Park was purchased by Sir William Hayter. This mansion was to be rebuilt at the end of the century in Bath stone and TLB bricks. In Eversley Charles Kingsley was rector of a small parish. He was best known for his book *The Water Babies*.

1860, the famous original mansion and hunting lodge built by William Trumbull was demolished, to be replaced by the present building, by the 2nd Marquess of Downshire, at Easthampstead Park.

1859, Wellington College was founded. The first 76 boys arrived on

20 January. The Rev. Edward White Benson was the first Master.

1863, Broadmoor received its first 95 female patients. The first Superintendant was Dr John Meyer, 1863–70. In 1864 the male patients arrived; amongst them was the artist Richard Dadd, who was to spend 22 years in Broadmoor. Bullbrook Church School was constructed in 1855. This school was in use for 126 years. Bullbrook was the oldest school building in Bracknell, originally a Sunday school belonging to Winkfield parish. When the first headmaster arrived, he found that his house was not ready, so he camped out in a tent for about seven weeks. It was replaced by yet another office block in 1985.

1856, the London and South Western Railway line was opened between Staines and Ascot, the station being only ten minutes' walk from the Grandstand. Ticket holders for the Royal Enclosure were entitled to use the path through the grounds of Ascot Heath House. Most of the area's local large mansions and houses were let for Ascot Race Week; so great was the demand for houses, the majority were secured months in advance.

1860, Thomas Lawrence moved to Bracknell and created the largest business in the district, employing hundreds of local people.

1870, Bracknell Market was established, where it was held weekly without a break in the yard behind the Hinds Head, until redevelopment. Frederick Hunton was the auctioneer, he was also estate agent and organist at Holy Trinity for 47 years.

1871, the picturesque route from Windsor to Ascot was spoilt by the dust from the road, spoiling coats and the lace dresses of the ladies.

1880, the Bracknell Cricket Club was founded.

1886, after the death of the Rev. C.P. Pratt, Canon H. Barnett came to Bracknell and introduced a weekly celebration of Holy Communion, replacing the monthly one.

1887, the Victoria Hall was built in Church Road, Bracknell, by public subscription to commemorate Queen Victoria's Jubilee.

1893, Wokingham's St Paul's Parish Room was built, complete with a magnificent clock tower. At the turn of the century, the Forest Hotel was built at the top of Bracknell High Street, on the site where a local bootmaker had his shop. The hotel was a commercial failure.

1901, Binfield Brick and Tile Works were built.

1903, *The Wokingham and Bracknell Gazette* was published from a press in the basement of a grocer's store in Denmark Street, Wokingham.

1908, the present Ranelagh School building was erected. Ranelagh School is the oldest existing institution in the parish, the original school was founded in 1709 by Richard, Earl of Ranelagh. Priestwood School was also built in 1908.

1910, in the general election campaign Ernest Gardiner, the Conservative candidate, successfully defended his seat by beating the Liberal candidate, Mr Knight.

1920, open-topped omnibuses were passing through Bracknell from Ascot to Reading.

1930, the Holt School for girls was opened in Wokingham.

1934–7, the Regal Cinema was opened in Bracknell. There was the Ritz in Wokingham, and Crowthorne High Street also had a cinema, which was lost in a fire and never rebuilt.

1934, Bracknell egg packing station was opened, which sold upwards of 120,000 eggs every week.

1937, King Edward VIII abdicated. King George VI and Queen Elizabeth were crowned on 12 May 1937. The local schoolchildren receive coronation mugs. Bracknell celebrations included the crowning of Miss Hilda Slade as Coronation Queen, by the Marchioness of Downshire.

1939, war declared against Germany.

1940, arrival of trainloads of evacuees, fleeing the terrible bombing of London, 1940–4.

1940, between July 1940 and May 1941 some 1,595 bombs and incendiaries were dropped in the county.

1943, a daylight bombing raid on Reading. The British Restaurant, known as the 'People's Pantry', received a direct hit, killing and injuring many people.

1945–6, peace returned to the world, but rationing continued until the early 1950s for some items.

1947, 10 July, the engagement was announced between Princess Elizabeth and Prince Philip of Greece. The royal wedding took place in Westminster Abbey on the morning of 20 November 1947. As clothing coupons were still in existence, the bride-to-be was obliged to save her coupons for the gown.

1948, 14 November, the birth of Prince Charles.

1949, a public meeting took place in the Victoria Hall, when Mr Lewis Silkin, Minister of Town and Country Planning, explained the government's plans to build a New Town in Bracknell.

1950, on 15 August 1950, HRH Princess Anne was born.

1952, on the night of 5–6 February, our beloved King George VI died.

1953, Queen Mary died in March. Hundreds of floral tributes were laid out in the grounds of Windsor Castle for the public to see.

1953, 2 June, the Coronation of Queen Elizabeth II. Bracknell crowned its own Coronation Queen, which was followed by street parties and processions.

1959, Bracknell's only centenarian, Mrs Annie Stoner, celebrated her 101st birthday at her home, St Catherine's, Ralphs Ride, Bracknell.

1960, HRH Prince Andrew was born on 19 February.

1960–70, Bracknell Old High Street was bulldozed, to make room for modern redevelopment.

1964, saw the birth of the Queen's last son, HRH Prince Edward.

1974, 20 March. A gunman was foiled in his attempt to kidnap Princess Anne in the Mall. Several people with the Princess were shot and injured.

1970–80, saw the almost total disappearance of Bracknell Old Town.

OLD BRACKNELL

The description of Bracknell in *Kelly's Directory* as being situated in a woodland country, the scenery very beautiful, was still true in my childhood. The difference being that the woodland parts hid the wartime ammunition dumps that we knew were there, but luckily the enemy didn't. Our Sunday afternoons were often spent in woodland or farmland walks, whichever took our fancy for some exercise after our Sunday lunch. It is a pity that today's generation of children cannot see the past beauty of this area, but we can take a trip down memory lane.

It would be nice to be able to turn the clock back in time, to before any of us were born, and try to picture this areas as our Bronze Age ancestors must have seen it.

The wild country hereabouts was inhabited, as evidence of prehistoric Man can be found around Bracknell, with the burial barrows of Bill Hill and towards the southwest of Wooden Hill in Easthampstead. These bowl barrows, dating back to our Bronze Age, as far back as 2,000 BC contain flint arrowheads, bones and drinking cups etc. from that time in our history.

At the time of the Roman invasion, our summer climate gave a warmer welcome to these shores than the chilly summers we have experienced since the Second World War. The Romans must have found our balmy climate very refreshing in this green and pleasant land. Small settlements were established around Berkshire, as the Roman roads progressed. One of these was explored in 1878 by the boys of Wellington College, who unearthed a large amount of bricks, pottery and broken tiles. Personal items were also uncovered, such as rings, brooches and bangles. Fragments of Roman earthenware vessels have also been ploughed up by many Berkshire farmers, but unfortunately more were broken up by the ploughs than were saved.

Our most historical monument is the Iron Age fort now called Caesar's Camp, which is on a 400- foot-high outcrop of land, shaped like an oakleaf. This earthwork was made long before the Roman invasion, and as yet has not been professionally excavated. As one walks over this old fort, one wonders what secrets may lie hidden beneath its soil.

As the Romans built their roads close by, they may well have used this old fort as a camp, although historians cannot agree on this point.

The great Roman military road from London to Silchester is now known as 'The Devil's Highway', for some unknown reason. It is a pity that so many Roman roads have disappeared under farmland, but they are still clearly visible from the air, built in straight, direct lines across the country from town to town.

These roads were built in most part by soldiers of the legions, with maybe local slaves doing the heavy work. They were made to last; the earth was rammed down hard, with alternate layers of clay and stones, and built up to a thickness of three to four feet and finished off with a further layer of flints or large flat stones. A ditch was dug along each side to drain off the water.

Our cold winters here in Berkshire must have been unpleasant for the Roman invaders. As many of them came from the Near East, or southern Italy, they were used to hot sunshine, not the snow and ice of England.

We were told in school lessons that the Nine Mile Ride straight road was Roman in origin, but some authors think that Queen Anne made the ride when she became riddled with gout, which made it impossible for her to ride a horse any more. But P.H. Ditchfield, in his book *The Byways in Berkshire and the Cotswolds*, thought that George III made this road. As to who was right in this matter, your guess is as good as mine. It could have been laid on top of an old existing road, thereby having a firm foundation to start with. Roman or not, the road is very straight for most of its nine-mile length, but what a different picture it paints today, with local traffic speeding along, and drivers who seem not to have a minute to live. In my girlhood, we often cycled along this quiet road, hardly meeting a soul, peddling along the centre of the road, with only the birds for company and the occasional rabbit sitting munching at the roadside, the air heavy with the aroma of the pine trees, especially on warm days.

When the Romans left Britain, the forests were safer places to live in, as the wild bears and packs of wolves had been hunted and killed, making peaceful grazing lands for cattle and sheep. Our part of Berkshire returned to wild heathland once more, until a Saxon settlement was set up. The Saxons lived off game of all kinds, and cultivated the sandy soil where possible. The Saxon name of Lachen-stede later became known as Easthampstead, after many name changes through the centuries. In the year 942, the name Braccan heal appeared where Bracknell now stands. All part of Windsor Forest, where generations of kings and queens spent their leisure hours hunting the wild game, unfortunately hunting the wild boar to extinction. Herne the Hunter was one of the most remembered huntsmen of all times, probably due to the many sightings of his ghost still

14

haunting the Forest of Windsor. Henry VIII was once much alarmed by the sudden appearance of Herne the Hunter.

Henry's first wife, Catherine of Aragon, spent a miserable existence at Easthampstead, awaiting the divorce from Henry, to which she was strongly opposed. Catherine also spent some time there after her divorce, but at least she managed to keep her head. James I made many improvements to the park. The John Norden survey maps he commissioned give us an excellent picture of the forest divided into 16 'walks', each with its own keeper. Each walke contained either fallow deer or red deer. Norden's map shows Old Bracknell and New Bracknell situated in 'Warfielde Walke'.

Many parts of the forest were in fact large areas of wild heathland. These became the haunt of many highwaymen, who made a living by robbing wealthy travellers, especially on Bagshot Heath. We were told many a tale of highwaymen at school, including Dick Turpin, William Davies, the 'Golden Farmer', who paid all his debts with gold coins, and the most famous, Claude Duval, who was noted for his chivalry. Not so Dick Turpin, who was a violent man, so unlike his character as portrayed on television and in films.

All three of these highwaymen were eventually caught and hanged, but not before William Davies spent 42 years as a highwayman, while at the same time leading a double life as a farmer in Gloucestershire, hence the name of the Golden Farmer.

Wokingham, too, suffered its plague of outlaws through the eighteenth century. The Wokingham Blacks were a notorious gang of poachers led by Will Shorter, a farmer, who blacked their faces and terrorised the local forest neighbourhood, extorting blackmail and even committing murder. They were brought to justice by the 'Black Act', a special Act of Parliament which made 'blacking' a felony. After a trial at Reading, the gang of four were hanged in chains on the heathland. There were gibbets at each corner of Windsor Forest during this period.

Bracknell had its own wicked landlord of the Hinds Head, who robbed and then murdered his guests by setting a bedside trap over a deep well, drowning the unsuspecting victims. The landlord was outwitted by a farmer, who was told of his impending danger by a chambermaid. An assault party of local farmers was organised, so the landlord and his gang of ruffians were captured and convicted, suffering the same fate as the highwaymen. The bones of their past victims in the well proved their guilt of these awful crimes. The young chambermaid must have been a brave bonny lass in bringing these robbers to justice, at the peril of her own safety.

In 1759 the Windsor Forest Turnpike Trust was created. The new improved Turnpike Road helped Bracknell develop into a main trading village. The coaching trade also was to benefit as roads were improved. Several of the old coaching inns can still be seen today, the Rose in Wokingham, and the Red Lion in Bracknell being just two examples. On the seventeenth-century maps, the High Street in Bracknell was just known as 'Bracknell Street'. The gentry must have found Bracknell a pleasant place to live, as many of their mansions began appearing in the area, and at Binfield, Warfield and Easthampstead.

I have a print of '*Mill Farm*' *Bracknel*, dated 1815. I don't know if Bracknell was spelt this way at the beginning of the nineteenth century, or if it is just a misprint.

The Old Mill House stood amongst woodland on the edge of Mill Pond. In a recent newspaper cutting that I have, there is a story that the mill was haunted and that the villagers were afraid to go near it. I had never heard of this story before, so we were quite happy during our many strolls around Mill Pond as youngsters. But my sister said that she thought the area always had an eerie feel about it. The pond was very still and silent, in a brooding kind of atmosphere of years ago, due to its remote and lonely location out in the woodlands. This silence was only broken by the low whistling sound of the breeze through the reeds and bullrushes around the water's edge. One could sit by the pool and actually listen to the silence.

Through the years I have been told many ghost stories of Bracknell's past and I think they deserve a mention later on separately. People who do not believe in ghosts, my mother being one of them, can then skip the chapter about them. But I myself have an open mind on this subject after an eerie experience in a house we once looked over, when our home was to be compulsorily purchased. Needless to say, we didn't buy the house in question.

Back in the early 1800s, Bracknell had three fairs a year: one in April, the next in August, and the last in October, which was also a hiring fair. Mothers who had youngsters of working age would go to these fairs to find employment for their children, the girls as servants in the homes of the gentry, and the boys as stable lads or gardeners and farm labourers etc. Whatever employment they found, life was to be hard-working from the moment that they grew out of childhood. The famous Bracknell fairs included cockfighting and the even more barbaric bull-baiting. These awful practices were banned in 1835, which was just as well, but not before local people were killed and injured during these cruel sports. In 1794 the victims of the Christmas bull-baiting in Wokingham were Elizabeth North, who was found dead, dreadfully bruised, and a man who had also been taken from

Old Mill House, Old Mill Lane, Easthampstead, in 1815

the bull without hopes of life. The coroner at the inquest found Elizabeth 'accidentally killed'.

In 1813 an Act was passed to enclose Windsor Forest, although it took a good many years to complete the enclosure. The appearance of the Crown Lands changed completely with the planting of pine trees over a large area. The almshouses built in 1760 by William Watts

Bridesmaids arriving at Holy Trinity for a 1930s wedding

17

opposite Easthampstead Church were demolished in 1826 by the Marquess of Downshire, who built new ones, which in turn were rebuilt to form the enlarged Union Workhouse after the Poor law Act of 1834 stated that paupers must enter workhouses to claim poor relief. It was still called 'the Union' when I was very young, but soon after became Church Hill House Hospital, as it is today.

The clock tower on the Union building was originally promised by the Marquess of Downshire for the bell tower of the church. But one Sunday as his Lordship arrived for church service, his stove-pipe hat was knocked from his head by a low bough of the enormous yew tree that stands to this day by the south entrance of the church. The Marquess ordered that the offending bough should be cut down, and was very put out when this order was not carried out. Feelings ran high, with the result that the fine clock ended up on the Union building instead of the church.

What a blessing that the fine old yew tree was saved by Reverend

Local brides of 1945 and 1983 walking under the yew tree the Marquess wanted axed

18

Townsend, as it still forms a pleasing archway under which many a pretty local bride has walked into church, and yes, it is still claiming a few hats to this day if one doesn't duck down low enough under its boughs. My own veiled hat ended up dangling on its branches at a wedding; luckily nobody caught the incident on the wedding films.

The beautiful memorial window to Caroline, Marchioness of Downshire, depicting Faith, Hope and Charity, has been completely ruined by the construction of an annex, which shuts out all light from this lovely window. It also seems a pity that some young people cannot leave these lovely old memorials for future generations to see. The vandals have repeatedly broken the 'Chetwynd Windows' in Bracknell's Holy Trinity Church, named after Charles Richard Blauw Chetwynd, assistant curate, who died in 1891, aged 28. Why this young man's memorials should be a target of these souls is beyond

(Easthampstead Church)

19

The first artist's impression of Bracknell Church. It was enlarged in the 1860s and the walls and lych-gate were added in the early 1900s

comprehension. I noticed on a recent visit to Binfield Church that it, too, had been the victim of the vandals. The 1980s will certainly be remembered by our descendants as the mindless years.

The brass memorial plaques in the church are also of interest. There is one for Lucie Lawrence, who died as a young girl, was a Sunday school teacher, and one for Richard Tranter, who lost his life on HMS *Pathfinder*.

Just two organists held the post for a century, Mr F. Hunton for 47 years, and Mr F.C. Faulkner for over 50 years. These plaques have now been joined by that of Mr Eric Few, who took over from Mr Faulkner. Mr Few died in June 1986 while working in the churchyard. He is sadly missed after his years of devotion to the church choir, and the beautiful floral arrangements in the church over many years.

Of the recent vicars of Bracknell, the Rev. F.L. Sugget only spent 21 months at the Holy Trinity. His stay as a missionary in South Africa was also short in duration. The Rev. G. Bond took over in 1933, but also resigned in August 1935. The Rev C. Anders' stay was longer in duration, from August 1935 to April 1947. He was followed

Local wedding fashions through the years.

Frederick and Gertrude (late 1800s)

Edward and Lily (1920s).

Edward became a Wokingham councillor

Michael and Diana (1930s)

Greville and Cynthia (1950s)

But the Holy Trinity Church servers, with the Rev. F.L. Sugget in 1933, look much the same

by the Rev. J. Fisher, who died on 5 December 1950. Then came the Rev. F. Broome, who saw the change of Bracknell from a small market town to the large new town of today.

It is a great pity that the developers have seen fit to isolate the church by building a ring road at the back, and a dual carriageway at the front, making the arrival of wedding and funeral cars a difficult task for all concerned., The lych-gate has been moved from front to back, leaving the lovely long path leading nowhere. Only modern development would leave a path leading into a brick wall.

Many villagers turned up for the weddings in days gone past, lining the church walls, waiting for a glimpse of the bride after the service, especially if it was the wedding of a well-known family.

A wild and lonely tract of heathland, known as the Aneth by locals, was a favourite place to lose oneself or a picnic or just for a stroll. What is now a dual carriageway of speeding vehicles was once a sandy little footpath meandering through purple heather and rhododendrons.

Amongst the bright yellow gorse bushes one could glimpse the pretty pink-breasted linnets or stonechats, while in the silver birch

In the 1960s, with the Rev. F. Broome. In fact, J. Young, who ran the gents' outfitters in the High Street, and the verger, F. Langley (the author's father) are in both pictures

trees the cuckoo sat calling his distinctive sound, which is so rarely heard in Bracknell any more.

My friend and I spent many a weekend strolling over this lonely sandy heathland which was the habitat of lizards and snakes, which could sometimes be seen sunning themselves on the sandy track. We never worried about them as we sat amongst the heather while the breeze rustled the previous year's dead rusty red bracken fronds. Like Mill Pond, this was an isolated spot where one could wander at will, enjoying the loneliness and solitude of yesteryear.

Harmans Water was a pretty little pool surrounded by dense rhododendrons and tall firs which reflected in its still waters. A little island over the opposite side with tall firs on it added to the beauty of this secretive hidden little pool.

Gormoor Pond, much larger and open in appearance, was also surrounded by rhododendrons, which reflected in its waters in May. This pond had lovely water lilies floating on its surface from July onwards. Its close proximity to Caesars Camp and the Romano–

British settlement, and further south The Devils Highway, make this large area the most interesting in our local history.

Dry Pond was another favourite picnic spot in our teens. Its tendency to dry out in hot summers was how it came by its name. It was situated on the Bracknell to Crowthorne road, where St Margaret Clitherow School and playing field are now.

From our home it was a nice walk along the Old Crowthorne Road, passing the wallabies jumping about in the field behind Coopers Hill House, and on past the Green Man public house, where just around the bend the lovely view of Easthampstead Church could be seen across the golden cornfields. Walking on down the hill, we climbed over the stile and went up through the cornfield to the church. Now we turned right to go down the steep hill and into winding Mill lane, before climbing over a stile and going along a footpath leading off into the bluebell woods. Through the silent woodlands we followed the millstream on its meandering course, where cuckoo pints and marsh marigolds grew in the dampness, and onto the fallen tree which acted as a bridge over the millstream to the stile by the pool. Years ago, this was a secret hiding place for all kinds of wildlife and water-fowl nesting amongst the reeds at the water's edge. The modern improvements around the pond have given it a rather sterile look, but the old pond is still bringing enjoyment to the children who boat on it.

The oldest building left standing in Bracknell is the Old Manor, also known in days gone by as Turpins Cottage, from the days of Dick Turpin, who also visited the Hinds Head. The Old Manor was the haunt of highwaymen, as were other inns in Berkshire, Bagshot Heath being a favourite hunting ground for these men of the road. Secret tunnels led from this building underground to the Hinds Head, and locals speak of a much longer one which emerged back up on open ground north of Clay Lane, now called Park Road.

A large house called High Elms was built later at the top of Park Road, and it was behind this property that the exit of this other tunnel was reputed to have been.

Another tunnel was rumoured to have been found under the Forest Hotel, formerly a bootmaker's shop. A friend told me of being shown the bricked-up tunnel exit down under the Forest when she was young; she found the experience rather creepy, so didn't explore it very much, but now wished that she had.

Recent rumours have had these tunnels leading all over the town, which is a pity, including the church, which wasn't built until two to three centuries later. I have also read misleading accounts of tunnels leading to the Bull, which is also of a later period, and even out towards the Horse and Groom in Bagshot Road. Maybe the present landlords think it will bring in extra custom for them by embroidering on the stories of the tunnels, but this spoils the authenticity of the original escape passages, which after all may not have been used by highwaymen at all, but by priests in different periods of history. A priest's hole in the Manor was so expertly concealed that it wasn't discovered until this century, when building work was carried out in recent years. The same kind of discovery was made in Whynscar, which is situated a short distance away from the Manor, a few yards west down the Old High Street. This was the home of the dental surgeon Mr T. Billington and his wife, who appeared in a newspaper report as 'looking up a priest's hole', which was a rather inappropriate piece of reporting, and caused a lot of amusement in their family.

The true purpose of these hidden passageways we shall never know, but for a town which supposedly has no history, this proves otherwise. Maybe the ghost of the priest or monk in Kells House in Church Road could have given us the answer, but he might be quite a recent spectre, as the first Roman Catholic Iron Church building wasn't erected until 1893 in Stanley Road. Before this time, monks came to Bracknell from Farnborough each Sunday, using a room in Kells House lent by the owner, a Mr Reilly. So perhaps the ghost dates from this period.

The stories of the tunnels being used by highwaymen is a more exciting tale, and the one which is preferred by the local landlords.

The time of the Tudors was a dangerous period in history for men of the cloth, and later a different situation when Royalists and Parliamentarians prepared for civil war. Many secret hiding places were built into the fabric of old buildings, not to be discovered until centuries later.

If a tunnel had led out as far as the Horse and Groom, it would have been unearthed when the railway was built, also subsequent building down the Old High Street would have found a tunnel if it led to the Bull, and as the church was not built until 1851 in Victoria's reign, it is also very doubtful that a tunnel led in that direction to a non-existent church,

As a child, I went to Red Cross classes which were held in two small rooms in The Forest Hotel, facing the old Hinds Head. My eldest sister attended a youth club which was held in other rooms of this lovely old building. The boys, for a dare, one day took us down some old back stairs into the basement, where we discovered some old carriages that had remained there long after the days of horse-drawn carriages had passed by. Whether they were left there by Doctor Fielden when motor cars took the place of horse-power, or whether they were left behind from way back from the hotel days, I do not know. But I have often wondered what happened to them when the Forest was pulled down. I hope they have been restored somewhere to their former glory, and not destroyed along with everything else that was Old Bracknell.

I was always a rather shy child, but the local lads were more adventurous and bolder than we girls. But for them, I would never have seen the carriages, having a quick glimpse before running back up the stairs again for fear of being told off for venturing down there in the first place. The boys seemed to have none of these fears, and ventured into the back of High Elms one day, which had stood empty for years. Finding a back door unlocked, they crept inside an old back kitchen. I was scared, so only stood on the threshold in case anyone should come. Its state of neglect made the old house all the more exciting. It seemed to be stored with all old furniture, and had large wooden shutters at the windows, as did other large houses of this period. But the others lost their nerve and did not venture far inside either, as the large old house stood very silent, with cobwebs majestically draped in all of the windows, and a layer of dust everywhere. With the shutters over the windows to keep out the sunlight, it must have been in total darkness, but for the tiny cracks giving a small shaft of light here and there. Which was probably why the boys didn't venture inside after all, as it would have seemed rather creepy. I felt safer in the garden, which was a tangled mass of undergrowth, out of which peeped beautiful old roses and lilacs, and a few other flowering shrubs which were bold enough to bloom in this wilderness. It was behind this old property that the longest tunnel from the Old Manor was rumoured to emerge back up into open ground again.

I used to find the overgrown gardens of the Forest equally charming. By the old ballroom was a walled-in garden, which in its dilapidated state fascinated me, and the fields where my friend and I spent so many happy summer days were once grass tennis courts and large lawns. But here the remains of the gardens could still be seen amongst the weeds. There was an abundance of rhododendrons and buddleias. Also pretty flowering shrubs and trees, including cherry, lilac and laburnum. Different roses were scattered here and there, many of which had reverted back to dog roses, which didn't worry us, as we thought them just as pretty in their wild state as the cultivated ones. The once lush lawns were now covered in buttercups, daisies, vetch and a few poppies here and there. This was a little girls paradise, where Audrey and I spent hours gathering flowers and watching hundreds of butterflies flitting to and fro. In our garden now, I think it lucky if I manage to spot six butterflies in a morning.

27

We didn't help by catching the cabbage whites, as they laid too many eggs on our wartime vegetable patch

It was while we were sitting in the field one day that, on hearing an aeroplane which seemed rather low, looking up, we saw hundreds of silver streamers floating down towards us sitting in the field. We as children didn't fully understand what was happening. The pretty silver strips were now scattering downwards all over the trees and field. The yellow laburnums took on the look of tinselled Christmas trees, and the field of buttercups was strewn all over with silver streamers. We ran around the field happily gathering up armfuls of the silver strips, which were now everywhere. I cannot remember my mother's reaction when on my return home she was presented with this useless pile of silver foil. But Father seemed more interested as he examined my 'prize' find. But I didn't really understand even when they mentioned the word 'Radar'.

The Forest was a very large hotel for a village the size of Bracknell. It was only full on Ascot Race Week, so consequently it was a financial failure for the owners. Later Doctor Fielden purchased the property as a home, and for use as a surgery. There was a stable block at the back, with residences for staff above, and at the entrance on the London Road. It was quite a large property for a country doctor. After Dr Fielden left, it was used as a hospital for a short spell during the war, and later for youth and other clubs of various kinds. The old building had been used by many people before the Corporation saw fit to pull this old landmark down, along with its clock, which could be seen from vantage points around the town.

It was through this period of change from Victoria's to Edward's reign that my grandparents were all leading different working lives in the surrounding areas of Crowthorne, Wokingham and Ascot. Although only working-class people, their way of life was interesting as they chose completely different occupations. But for young women the choice was not so varied, and most had to go into service on leaving school. A hard life, of long working hours, with very little time off.

But before I write about my grandparents, I want to tell you about some of the famous – and infamous – people connected with Bracknell and Berkshire.

BULLBROOK

Through the Warren, I wander along,
Singing as I go my babbling song.
By Ralphs Ride, and under the bridge,
Where children play, up on the ridge.

Across Broad Lane, I go on my way,
Every night, and every day.
Behind the houses, and near to the school,
Where children paddle, and play the fool.

Catching small tiddlers, in tiny jam jars,
Then taking them home, to poor mammas.
Across London Road, to the old Royal Oak,
Along Bay Road, where boys sail little boats.

To be thrown in was such a shocker,
Living close by, you were a proud Bullbrook Docker.
Alas! In Bracknell, I am seen no more,
The name of Bullbrook is now folklore.

Bay Road

The Aneth

THE HIGHWAYMEN

The Civil War of the seventeenth century drove many men to take to the roads for High Toby. Having his estates confiscated, Philip Stafford, who was born about 1622 in the Newbury area, became the highwayman known as 'Captain Stafford'. He operated mostly in Maidenhead Thicket, and was caught after robbing a farmer on the Reading road. After his trial he made a desperate attempt to escape, which failed. On his execution day he had a drink with the hangman, promising to pay 'on his way back'.

Claud Duval was hanged at Tyburn in 1670. He was a man who was noted for his chivalry, especially to the ladies. Claud often held up coaches on Bagshot Heath, and was reputed to have hideouts in our locality.

Francis Jackson was hanged in chains on Hampstead Heath after being shot in the arm during a robbery in 1674. He waited with three accomplices in Maidenhead Thicket to no avail, then they made their way singly into Reading, where they were well known at the local inn. A gentleman who was staying in the inn at this time was later robbed on his way to Marlborough.

William Davis, known as the 'Golden Farmer' spent 45 years leading a double life as a respected churchgoing farmer, and highwayman. Davis retired for a while, then unwisely became greedy for more land, robbing a coach to gain the money for this purpose. He was recognised and was shot in the back. William was 64 years of age when he was later hanged on Bagshot Heath in 1690, and was the father of 18 children.

Sir John Popham of Littlecote, near Hungerford, operated as a highwayman for ten years, before being persuaded by his wife to settle down. Later as a famous Lord Chief Justice, he condemned many of his old accomplices.

Born at the Bell Inn at Hempstead in Essex in 1705 was one Richard Turpin. As a butcher, Turpin received stolen deer poached from the local forests. Turpin soon joined a gang of no less than 15 men, led by Samuel Gregory. The gang raided many farmhouses, where the owners were beaten and burnt to make them reveal the whereabouts of their best valuables.

Through the ten years of 1725–35 Turpin became a notorious outlaw, but even so, he gained shelter at many inns locally around

Windsor Forest and Bagshot Heath. There was a tunnel under the road leading from the Manor to the Hind's Head which was large enough to hide a rider mounted on his horse. (The landlord was reputed to drown his victims in the well under the inn.)

It is Turpin's ghost on Black Bess that is reputed to gallop down the London road east of Bracknell, turning left over the heathlands of the Old Ralphs Ride on his way to Bagshot Heath. Black Bess was stabled at many hideouts in Berkshire, and the Manor afterwards was known as 'Turpins Cottage'.

By 1732 Turpin had to keep moving to new territories, as his description was well known and he was noticeably marked by smallpox.

In February 1735, three of the gang were caught in the Punch House. Wheeler turned informer, with the result that three other members of the gang were caught and hanged. Two other members of the gang tried to escape to the Continent, but after a robbery near Godalming, they were apprehended at Hindhead.

Turpin spent some time in Holland, but was unwise enough to return in 1737. Leicestershire and Essex became his hunting grounds. Turpin had to hide in Epping Forest when another member of his gang was shot.

The rumour that he rode to York seems to be untrue. Swift John Nevison in 1676 robbed a sailor at Godshill at 4 a.m. then rode to York by 7.45 p.m. to give himself an alibi. This story later became muddled, in that it was Turpin who rode to York. But anyone driving to York will find both stories hard to believe, as many, many changes of horses would be needed for that long journey.

Turpin changed his name to John Palmer, but his handwriting on a letter to his brother in Essex was recognised by his old schoolmaster, and his captors in York then knew they had the right man in the cells. On 7 April 1739 Richard Turpin was hanged at Tyburn. Still showing off to the crowds to the last, he jumped from the ladder.

But is it Black Bess that is still to be heard galloping the turnpike road, now the London road, here in Bracknell?

FAMOUS MEN IN BERKSHIRE'S PAST

ALEXANDER POPE was born in London on 21 May, in 1688. A sickly child, he had a small and crooked infirm body, which shut him out of many youthful fellowships and activities.

The son of a prosperous draper, Alexander developed into a rather precocious young man. In his desire to become famous, he endeavoured to appear cleverer than he really was by pretending that some of his poems were written at an earlier age than they actually were. In this he appears vain, and a bit of a sneak.

In later years he was also liable to turn on his friends, and took great delight in attacking them with the most bitter satires.

In our strolls now over Popes Meadow in Binfield, we tend to think only of the romantic and poetic side of Alexander Pope, not of the weaknesses and jealousy that can affect even the most brilliant of minds. But it must be remembered that Alexander lived in an artificial age, when simple sincerity did not count.

He grew up in Binfield, and by the time that he was 26, he had published his *Windsor Forest, The Temple of Fame* and *The Rape of the Lock,* among many more juvenile poems. Later he was to spend 15 or so years writing bitter satires, which were unbecoming of him. A great pity.

Finally he wrote *An Essay on Man,* but it is for his *Essay on Criticism,* which was written when he was a youth of only 20, that he is best remembered. Alexander grew from sickly childhood into a great poet.

Here is a characteristic couplet from this essay:

> A little learning is a dangerous thing;
> Drink deep, or taste not the Pierian spring.

PERCY BYSSHE SHELLEY was born at Warnham in Sussex in 1792. Shelley in his youth was not happy at home and became a rebel against authority, somewhat like some youth of today. But Shelley was socially well born, and this rebel attitude led to him having to leave Oxford. He married young, and after this marriage foundered, his wife committed suicide. Shelley spent a period of his youth here in Bracknell, and used to sail little paper boats across the ponds while daydreaming, maybe with the future in mind, when he would sail away from England's shores. Shelley rowed across the pond in Braybrook, in an old tub, just to win a wager. A dangerous prank, and maybe an omen of his future fate from drowning. He wrote *Queen Mab* while residing in Bracknell in 1812–13.

When Shelley was 25 he left England, and produced beautiful poems abroad. His second wife was Mary, who became well known as the authoress of *Frankenstein*. Shelley was a great friend of the sixth Lord Byron, and together they roamed through the most beautiful scenery of the Adriatic.

A few lines of Shelley's 'Julian and Maddalo' reads:

> This ride was my delight, I love all waste
> And solitary places, where we taste
> The pleasure of believing what we see
> Is boundless as we wish our souls to be.

The body of Shelley was cast up on the shore near Spezzia in Italy in 1822. He was only 29.

It is unclear where Shelley lived or stayed here in Bracknell, but in years gone by there was a 'Shelley's Cottage' in Easthampstead, long since vanished or gone. Byron, along with Leigh Hunt and Trelawny, burned the sad remains of Shelley, and took his ashes to Rome, to rest by the grave of Keats. A beautiful memorial to Shelley can be found in Christchurch Priory.

OSCAR FINGAL O'FLAHERTIE WILLS WILDE was born on 16 October 1854, the second son of William and Jane Wilde. His middle-class family lived in Dublin, where his great-great-grandfather was a merchant, his great-grandfather was a farmer at Castlereagh, and his grandfather was a physician. Oscar's father followed his grandfather's profession, and founded St Mark's Hospital in 1844. His father's three brothers all became priests.

Oscar's father had three illegitimate children before his marriage. The old Regency permissiveness lingered on in Dublin at that time. It seems that no one minded about this way of life. A boy named Henry Wilson was born in 1838. This illegitimate son later became a fellow practitioner in his father's surgery. Two illegitimate girls were born, the mothers unknown, Emily in 1847, and Mary in 1849. These two girls were adopted by Oscar's uncle, the Rev. Ralph Wilde, as his wards. The Wildes' legitimate daughter, named Isola, was only nine years old when she died of a fever in February 1867.

The death of his little sister affected Oscar deeply, and he wrote the following poem:

Tread lightly, she is near
Under the snow.
Speak gentle, she can hear
The lilies grow.

All her bright golden hair
Tarnished with rust,
She that was young and fair
Fallen to dust.

Lily-like, white as snow
She hardly knew
She was a woman so
Sweetly she grew.

Coffin-board, heavy stone
Lie on her breast
I vex my heart alone
She is at rest.

Peace, Peace, she cannot hear
Lyre or sonnet,
All my life's buried here
Heap earth upon it.

Oscar Wilde had connections with the area and called his most famous character Lady Bracknell

A tragic fate also awaited poor Emily and Mary. While showing off their ballgowns, one got too close to the fire and went up in flames. Her sister frantically tried to save her, in vain. Both girls died on 10 November 1871, just four years after their little half-sister Isola.

It was while he was at Portora, Oscar's dandyism and adoption of Hellenism became more apparent. After Oscar's brother left Dublin to study law in London in 1872; Oscar also left Ireland for Oxford in 1874. His flamboyant clothes and extravagant behaviour at Oxford vexed his parents and tutors alike. He was to spend the future walking a tightrope between respectability and dissipation. He cared little for others' feelings, but appeared very hurt at any recrimination against himself.

His father died on 19 April 1876. His mother had permitted a veiled visitor to sit at her dying husband's bedside, maybe the mother of his illegitimate children.

In March–April 1878, Wilde believed that he had contracted syphilis, for which he took mercury, hopeful of a cure. Earlier he had fallen for the charms of Florence Balcome, whom he hoped to marry, but this became impossible, as he had a two-year wait before his syphilis cure was complete. Later this first love of Oscar's married Bram Stoker, future author of *Dracula.*

In 1877–78 Wilde was judged to be best of his year by examiners in Final Schools, and had also been awarded the Newdigate Prize. The dons were astonished at the bad boy coming good in the end. Later he passed his examination of divinity.

After two years had gone by, Oscar was still upset over the loss of Florence Balcombe, and wrote several poems of dejection. He applied for several posts in Oxford, which had replaced Dublin in his heart, but failed to get any of them.

Four years later, in 1884, Wilde became engaged to Constance Lloyd, a pretty girl with violet eyes. They were married at St James Church on 28 May, the bride in a gown, designed by Oscar, of rich satin of cowslip tint, with a wreath of myrtle leaves and white blossoms in her hair.

Cyril, their first child, was born on 5 June 1885, and the following year, on 5 November, their second son Vyvyan was born. His parents changed the date to 3 November 1886, so that it wasn't Guy Fawkes Day. Whereas other husbands rejoiced in their wives' pregnancies, Wilde found it rather distasteful. he soon grew tired of playing husband, and he and Constance gradually grew apart.

Oscar was eager for the society of young men. In 1886 he met Robert Ross and their affair carried on until 1888, the year *The Happy Prince* was published.

In 1891 Wilde became friendly with Lord Alfred Douglas, who was the son of the Marquess of Queensberry. This friendship was to cause his downfall. In 1887, *Kelly's Directory* shows that the Marquess of Queensberry was residing at Easthampstead.

In 1892, Lady Queensberry was very disturbed at her son's homosexual affair with Oscar Wilde, and asked him to her house in Bracknell to discuss the matter. Her efforts were all in vain. The pair attended wild house parties in Bracknell, especially on Ascot race weeks.

Their affair became a big scandal. Oscar was deserted by many friends, but never quite completely by Constance.

The Marquess of Queensberry accused Oscar Wilde of being a sodomite. Urged on by Alfred Douglas Oscar sued for criminal libel, but his case collapsed. He was arrested and ordered to stand trial, and was sentenced to two years' hard labour in May 1895. *The Ballad of Reading Gaol* was written about this period.

Oscar was appalled at the plight of three little children, who were thrown into Reading Gaol for snaring a rabbit. Also of a poor man who was mentally ill and was flogged for supposedly malingering. His shrieks could be heard in his cell. Constance Wilde changed her name to Holland, to protect her sons. Oscar was released from gaol in May 1897. He remained more or less a broken man, and died, some believed from the effects of syphilis, on 30 November 1900.

A few miles down the road, just over the Hampshire border, lived an entirely different kind of man, quiet and gentle, not at all flamboyant. He was CHARLES KINGSLEY – a name always remembered with affection, a gifted and true Christian man.

Charles was born in Devonshire, on 12 June 1819, the son of a clergyman. It was at Cambridge University that he distinguished himself.

His short curacy at Eversley was so successful that after the rector died, a campaign by the villagers for his return as their rector in 1844 ended with him remaining there for the next 31 years. His love of nature, his skilful swing of a flail amongst the threshers, and the

Author Charles Kingsley spent most of his life in nearby Eversley

turn of his swathe with the mowers in the meadows accounted for why he was so loved. One just can't imagine Wilde or Byron in their dandy clothes soiling their hands in country pursuits, as Charles Kingsley loved to do. His example was of the true kind-hearted Englishman.

Charles was a brilliant novelist. The first stories he penned were *Alton Locke* and *Yeast*, which showed his art in reaching the general public. But he will best be remembered for *The Water-Babies* and *Westward Ho!*

The vicarage garden was a place of rest and refuge in which to write his stories, and in earlier years he had sent vivid sketches and descriptions of it to the lady who was later to become his wife.

Two years before he died, Charles was appointed Canon of Westminster and Chaplain to Queen Victoria. He died on 23 January 1875.

Here was a fine example of a true-hearted Englishman, concerned for the religious and social well-being of his beloved England. Queen Victoria made a wise choice in Charles Kingsley as her chaplain.

MY GRANDPARENTS

My paternal grandparents met when Grandfather left his home town of Wokingham and went up to Bedfordshire to work at a large country house at the village where Granny lived. It was during this period that he met Gertrude, and fell in love with her. But it was the rule of his employers that staff should not mix with girls from the village. Gertrude was a village girl when they started courting, the end result being that Grandfather was dismissed. But I do not think that Frederick ever regretted his choice of Gertrude as his wife, as they remained devoted to each other throughout their married life, right up until Grandfather had a stroke which rendered him speechless and bedridden. Granny and my aunt nursed him devotedly until the end.

Grandfather devoted most of his early life to the care of horses as a groomsman. This love of horses continued until he was in the mounted artillery during the First World War. Granny found that

A local family in the First World War, with father and sons in uniform

two of her sons, as well as her husband, were in army uniforms during this period. So many local mothers lost their sons in that carnage – such a waste of young lives. But Grandfather came back from France safely, after many photographs and postcards had been sent home to

Many local men perished. The funeral of Naval Dispatch Rider Lionel Rainford

The procession for Alfred Davis of the Royal Berkshires

Four of those who returned.

Private John Scott ran Bracknell Market and Hunton's Estate Office

Trooper Harry Alder had a dairy herd, and his milking parlour was in Bull Lane

Private Albert Youens ran a cycle shop in the High Street

Corporal Bill Fowler organised whist drives in the Church House

Four Bracknell boys in the Berkshire Yeomanry met different fates at Hill 70. (Top) Lance Corporal E. Gale (wounded); Trooper A. Alcot; Trooper Philip Bowyer (killed) and Trooper Harry Alder (wounded)

the family. It was a practice during the war to send photographs home in the shape of postcards. The messages on the back were often brief and to the point: 'To Father from your loving Son Horace', the young son on the front looking no older than 15 or 16. Many lads added a couple of years on to their ages to join up. A return postcard from France of Grandfather on his charger, has an equally brief message, 'From your loving Father'. Nothing was mentioned of the hardships they were suffering in the mud and trenches of France. Another message from another son reads 'The simple truth, I am still alive, was vaccinated today'.

Sometime during the early part of their marriage, my grandparents made the move from Bedfordshire back down to Wokingham to live, where they brought up their family of five children. They lived out the rest of their lives in Wokingham, where in later years Grandfather became Sexton and Verger at All Saints Church for many years. This was in complete contrast to his earlier life spent in caring for horses. But taking pride of place on the sitting room wall was an oil painting of Prince Charming, a hunter which Grandfather groomed and looked after for many years. The painting was a gift from the owner. The

This window in Warfield Church is a memorial to Amey Butler, who was widowed in the First World War and had to bring up her six young daughters alone

shape of horses seems to have changed over the years: Prince Charming's head looks small in comparison to horses of today. He is painted in such a way that he appears to be looking at you out of one eye, no matter where you are in the room. As a youngster I used to try and hide from his gaze in different parts of the room, but it followed me around. The mark of a clever artist.

Grandmother's little house used to shine like a new pin. Girls took great pride in their homes after years in service in the country houses of the gentry. Which is why marriage was a fulfilling job, after their years of strict servitude were replaced by the pleasure of bringing up their own children. What a pleasant change it must have been from their past life, where every whim of the rich had to be attended to, otherwise it meant instant dismissal.

Sometimes workers got their own back in the strangest of ways, as was once witnessed by my father as a young boy. He had just started as a young gardener on a large estate, from which one of the head gardeners had been dismissed after an argument with his employer. Father later came up from behind this man in the conservatory one day, just in time to watch him pouring something around the roots of a very old grapevine. As father was just a young lad at the time, he was uncertain as to what he should so, so he stood quietly as the man crept away, unaware of his presence. Needless to say, the grapevine later died. Such was the fear of losing one's job in those days that Father kept knowledge of this incident to himself, only telling his family about it, for fear that he should be blamed instead.

It is funny to think of days gone past, when if a member of the gentry was ill and confined to bed, the roadway outside was covered in straw to deaden the sound of passing horses and carts etc. One wonders how they would cope in this modern world of Concorde, police sirens and heavy lorries. They must have had fragile and delicate constitutions in those days.

The peaceful days of horse-power to be envied in some ways, but not in others, especially in the case of fires, when little if anything could be done to stop them spreading. Many a local mansion was lost in this sad way. Sir George Dasent's house was destroyed at Tower Hill, Ascot, on 24 October 1890. Servants formed human chains, passing buckets of water, from hand to hand along the line to the seat of the fire. A frustrating and often hopeless task from the beginning for all concerned, who after a long battle to save a house could only at the end stand and watch helplessly as it burned to the ground. This sad fate awaited the Berystede at Ascot on the morning of 27 October 1886, when the home of the Standish family was destroyed by fire. The bones of Mrs Standish's French maid, Eliza Kleininger, were found at the foot of the servants' staircase. Although now rebuilt and used as a hotel, the Berystede has retained Eliza's ghost, on the north side of the hotel, where the old staircase used to be.

My Grandparents' small home is still standing next to All Saints Church in Wokingham, but here in Bracknell all of our homes have disappeared under the development of the New Town. As my maternal grandparents were dead, I loved being able to visit my paternal grandparents' home. Although Granny was a strict little lady, we all loved her dearly. But we were never allowed to play card games on a Sunday, and we had to walk, not run, upstairs in those days. On lifting Granny's curtains one day to see who was over the road, I was smartly told off at once. One should never move the curtains, as the neighbours might think that we were being nosey, and that would never do! I never gave her curtains even the slightest twitch after that. I amused myself by studying the many old photographs covering the walls, with hardly an inch to spare between them. The old wedding pictures of my parents and aunts and uncles were my favourites. The fashions of the 1920s looked so quaint to a child in the 1940s.

Little ornaments dating from Victorian times sat on every cupboard and shelf space. Dusting these must have been a big job each week. The polished tables were each covered in a heavy velvet tassle-edged tablecloth, to protect them from scratches and the bright sunlight. Even the mantelpiece was covered in a velvet cloth forming a tassle-edged pelmet around the front, a fashion long forgotten now. This best room was only used when visitors arrived. The small back parlour was the living room, with the old-fashioned kitchen range, highly polished with black lead, keeping this little room warm and cosy. There was a large old pendulum clock, with its loud *tick-tock* and the chimes striking every quarter of an hour. When the hourly strike came, these chimes were joined by others from all over the house. I loved Granny's striking clocks!

Houses before the war never had the back parlours plastered, or the sculleries and kitchens of this period. Where the women spent most of their working days, the walls were just painted, usually in two colours, cream at the top, with maybe the more serviceable colours of dark green or brown for the bottom half, which would receive the most knocks. Sometimes the dividing line was picked out with a carefully painted black stripe, about an inch wide. This called for a steady hand on behalf of the decorator. The sculleries or kitchens were only given a coat of distemper, which after the continual steam treatment of washing days would soon start to flake and fall off, looking very unsightly. How lucky we are today with our modern emulsion paints etc.

44

Every Monday the old brick boiler would be lit, ready for the mammoth task of the weekly wash. The scullery was so filled with steam that we often couldn't see poor Gran inside; she would emerge red-faced with her tin bath of spotless white linen to hang out on the line. I remember the old brown earthenware sinks, chipped through the years of heavy use, the enamel bowls also chipped with wear and tear.

Granny's kitchen contained just a well-scrubbed table and old-fashioned cooker – kitchen ranges were beginning to go out of use, being replaced by gas-fired cookers – and up on the shelves were shiny rows of pots and pans. But a kettle was still kept heated on the old range in the parlour, ready for visitors' cups of tea. The old flat heavy irons were also heated on the range on ironing day; she would give it a quick spit on the bottom to see if it was hot enough for ironing to commence. I cannot get my modern saucepans to shine like Granny's, but then saucepans were made to last a lifetime, and didn't have the handles working loose after a short while, but should a hole appear or a handle come loose, it would be kept in a handy place ready for when a travelling tinker called, who would soon put it right and mend it well enough to last another ten years. The trade of the tinkers has completely vanished in our wasteful throw-away age. If the tinker found that a pot could not be mended, it still would not be thrown away, but kept ready with other items for when the rag-and-bone man came to call. He was a favourite with the children, as his loud call of 'Any rags and bones?' could be heard coming from streets away. The loud *clip-clop, clip-clop* sound of his large carthorse would herald a mad scramble to find the things that had been kept for his arrival in our district. Everything was dropped for his coming, even if we were in the middle of our tea.

It was a good excuse to go out to pat and fondle his lovely old horse, who peered at us with brown eyes half hidden behind blinkers. We would beg Mum to give us some sugar lumps, or maybe an apple or carrot for the patient animal standing passively waiting, while the cart was loaded with the things thrown away by us, but which would still make a few coppers for the rag-and-bone man. With trembling outstretched flat palms of our hands, we would offer up our little morsels for the horse to eat, half afraid that he would gobble up our fingers in the process with his gigantic brown teeth. Standing back fascinated as the loud *scrunch, scrunch* showed us how much that he was enjoying his tit-bit, we were very proud of the fact that we had been brave enough to put our hands near his big teeth, as we didn't want to appear cowards in front of the rag-and-bone man's children. They who were so used to dealing with horses, who had been watching us with some amusement.

45

We children of different lifestyles stood eyeing each other with curiosity, rather than nosiness, as the adults chatted. We took in their plaited greased hair and rather heavy and often grubby clothing, due to their hard life, while in return their steady gaze seemed to take note of our starched gingham dresses, with our matching hair ribbons. In our grandparents' childhood, these travelling children would often be barefooted and ill-clad. Granny being a proud little lady would always give them clothes which were well laundered and mended. She would not have dreamt of giving them dirty or torn clothing, even if they ended up in that condition shortly after their new little owners had worn them for a few days.

The appearance of the rag-and-bone man's wife was even more fascinating to our eyes, with her plaited greased hair hidden under a curious high-crowned straw hat, and a large shawl covering her shoulders. She wore what seemed like several layers of skirts of differing lengths, and often this type of lady would be puffing away on a clay pipe, a habit that we just could not imagine our mother taking up. Under the long layers of skirts, stout hard-wearing boots could be seen on her feet, which were needed as these families must have walked miles each day earning a living.

Finally we would bid them farewell, while the old horse was coaxed backwards and forwards, with heavy stamping feet, as the cart had to be manoeuvred in a tight circle to go back up the lane again and out into Church Road. We returning to our half-eaten tea, while they trundled on to Rochdale Road, to our neighbours' house up the back garden, with the ever patient old horse waiting for the cart to become full, before being able to return to their campsite for a well-earned rest. As the cries of 'Any rags and bones?' grew fainter and fainter in the distance, I became a little sad with the thought that we might not see them again for months, even if the travelling children's steady gaze for some reason made me feel rather a cissy!

Another familiar sight was the knife-grinder on his specially adapted tricycle, peddling from village to village sharpening knives and scissors on his way. Neighbours would send the word around of his arrival, and all of the utensils that needed sharpening would be taken out for him to grind. The children of each road would gather around to watch him at work, fascinated as he peddled away, making the grinding wheel gather up speed, then in a flurry of sparks, the grinding work commenced. We would run out with extra old scissors and knives to sharpen, just to watch him work, spellbound for a little longer, before he eventually peddled off to the next street.

Another regular pedlar who called every year was the French onion seller. Wearing a little black beret on his head, he called from door to door, his bicycle heavily laden with strings of onions for sale. With his smattering of our English language, and Father's little smattering of French, picked up while serving in the army in Europe, they somehow managed a short conversation, amid lots of smiles when they could not make each other understand. These regular pedlars would be greeted as old friends each year by my parents and grandparents alike. All working-class people understood the others' need to make a living.

The travelling gypsies were another frequent visitor to our doors, with their baskets of pegs, lace and other odds and ends. They were not quite so welcome as the other pedlars, simply for the fact that if you could not afford to buy anything, and money was hard to come by in our parents' time, the hapless housewife was liable to receive a curse from the gypsy instead. But if on the other hand you could purchase something, one was often presented with a sprig of lucky white heather. A gypsy's curse or warning was taken seriously in the old days, and rather than risk receiving one, it was thought better not to answer the door if caught at a time when the last of the week's wages was needed for food.

Gypsy camps were a familiar sight around the outskirts of the Bracknell years ago. Strings of washing would be hung up to dry on a line tied up between two trees. Ponies were tethered nearby, grazing on the grass verges. Well-fed dogs would always be roaming around with them. Some of the true Romany caravans were a lovely sight to see. Brightly coloured designs covered the exteriors, while the interiors were beautifully polished, and many contained lovely brass ornaments and fittings. These gypsies could not be confused with the other travelling people, who were called Diddies; these were not so clean in their habits, and would often swindle or cheat for a living, giving the true gypsies a bad name.

Although life was a lot harder in our grandparents' time at the beginning of this century, without washing machines and electric irons etc, other wifely chores were a lot easier in some ways. Take shopping as a small example. All grocers, bakers, butchers, greengrocers and ironmongers had a delivery service to customers' doors. As well as these, for those who could afford them, there were the excellent laundry services. There were two very good laundries here in Bracknell, both off Broad Lane. With the arrival of washing machines in the home, the laundry businesses became redundant; as did small family grocers with the influx of giant supermarkets, which do not have delivery services that were such a help to busy housewives with young families, and older people. Our grandparents simply gave the delivery man the new order list of groceries for the following week, while at the same time paying for the goods just delivered.

The coalman was another regular visitor, humping their hundred-weight sacks of coal, with what seemed the greatest of ease, but in fact must have been one of the most tiring, as well as one of the dirtiest, jobs to carry out. If coal was delivered to the church, always by the ton, the poor coalmen had to carry their loads through the churchyard, then down winding stone steps and on through a narrow dark passageway to the boiler room deep under the lady chapel. Most times two coalmen would deliver, but this still meant ten journeys for each man. These delivery men became personal friends to all of their customers, and always seemed to carry out their work with a smile and cheerful greeting. None of the 'take it or leave it' attitudes of tradesmen now. These were the days of service with a smile. The coalmen were always honest and straight; we were never ever a sack short, as we children loved to count the number of sacks going past our window to the coalshed. Sadly, honesty seems a forgotten virtue now. Some friends who run a garden supply business in our modern times of plenty have to watch every customer, especially the ones with the largest cars, who load three sacks of garden peat into their boots and then try to pay for only one.

Our grandfather used to ring the 'curfew' bell at 8 p.m. each night. This was an old custom dating back to 1664, so that strangers would not lose their way in the countryside. The original will of Richard Palmer provided for the ringing of the bell at 4 a.m. as well, but I think that custom was dropped by Grandfather's time. The ringing of the bell at these hours marked the times when it was thought that all good people should rise in the mornings, and go to bed at night. It is a pity these old customs die out after keeping going for nearly 250 years or so, even if they now serve no useful purpose. People nowadays seem very intolerant of the beautiful sound of church bells, but on the other hand are quite prepared to put up with the noise of Concorde, heavy lorries and factory din.

We used to love popping through the hedge of Grandad's garden to wander around the churchyard next door, reading the quaint little verses on the tombstones in All Saints. but our favourite was the following inscription on the headstone of John Clark, who died in 1880, and is in Holy Trinity Churchyard.

> All people that are standing by,
> As you are now, so once was I,
> As I am now, so you must be,
> So do prepare, to follow me.

In our grandparents' day, women ceased going to work once the family arrived, unless the unfortunate woman was a widow; then the only jobs open to them was that of a cleaner or laundry women. None had full-time jobs, as their modern counterparts. It was a sad fact of life that teachers and nurses had to leave their employment once they got married. This situation would not be tolerated today. Having the choice of keeping one's job and staying single, or getting married, thereby losing it, must be one of the reasons why there seemed to be many more spinster ladies around in days gone past. Modern housewives couldn't cope with two jobs without the help of washing machines and vacuum cleaners etc. Gardening, which once was considered to be man's work, is quickly being taken over by the females of households.

The almost daily ritual of whitening the doorsteps and copper tops has died out. Early morning would find streets of housewives out whitening their front doorsteps and woe betide anyone who stepped on it before it had dried to a nice whiteness.

We loved playing in hayricks as children, until Uncle Bill poked one with a fork one day, just to watch our reaction when dozens of little mice scattered here and there.

We didn't have to lock our homes up like fortresses. The back doors were often left unlocked, even while we were out shopping. There wasn't the fear of homes being broken into years ago. Even if a pedlar called while a house was empty, he would just go on to the next house if there wasn't an answer to his knock. Working-class folk did not prey on their own kind. A man's home was his castle, however humble, and there wasn't the invasion of one's privacy as there is now, with house burglaries every week. This does not mean to say that there weren't villains around, but the dishonest members of society seemed to steal more from those who could afford it; although still dishonest, this was a little better than the repeated beatings of old folk now, sometimes for the sake of a few coins.

My husband's grandparents chose a totally different occupation to that of verger or a dormitory man etc. George Briggs was the proprietor of the Squirrel in Winkfield for many years, where my deceased father-in-law was born, along with his brothers and sisters. The family moving later to the Seven Stars at Blacknest Gate, now sadly renamed the Chukker.

One day as my grandparents were hurrying across one of Wellington's playing fields as a storm was brewing, carrying a basket of supplies between them, a bolt of lightning struck nearby and forked to the basket also, throwing Grandfather to the ground. Granny dropped the basket and ran, not knowing quite what had happened.

After the shock had passed, she found Grandfather had been pulled all down one side of his body by the lightning, from which I am glad to say that he recovered. But the shock of it took them awhile to get over. Granny once told my mother of another occasion in a storm, when she had watched as lightning travelled up a pair of her lace curtains, leaving it in two separate pieces. In another storm, a large tree was struck in the grounds of Wellington with such a force that the tree exploded, scattering pieces of shattered wood. The tree was completely destroyed. No wonder that my mother was always afraid of storms and hid under the stairs at the first clap of thunder. With our cooler summers now, storms do not appear as frequent as they once were.

My father, too, in later years, was to also have a close encounter with lightning during his days as Verger at Holy Trinity in Bracknell. He popped out of the vestry door after a wedding to see if it was safe for the bridal couple to go outside for the photographs to be taken, just at the very moment that the church tower was struck, bringing a shower of shingle down all around him on the church steps, where the couple would have been standing for their photographs. The lightning conductor took the force safely down into the ground, but not before Dad stood frozen to the spot as he watched the lightning play a pretty zigzag pattern all down the wall within inches of where he was standing. He rushed back inside to tell the bride and groom to wait awhile. During an earlier storm, the conductor had a fault in it halfway down the tower, and it was at this point during a bad storm, that the lightning forked, going into the tower and striking the mechanism of the clock, severing a thick steel bar into two pieces. The bride had a day to remember, but maybe not in the way that she had intended.

On another occasion during a wedding, it was such a windy day that the bride's veil took off, ending up hanging halfway up the church tower. But I cannot remember how they managed to retrieve it.

Going back to the days of grandmother's girlhood, most young women had to go into service in the large houses owned by the gentry. My grandmother had to leave her home town of Abingdon and go into service in a large house at Crediton in Devon. Their hours of work were very long, with only one Sunday afternoon off in a month, and they were all expected to attend church on Sunday as well. If during their long day, they needed to go up to their bedrooms for any reason, they had to ask the permission of the cook before doing so. As their tiny rooms were situated in the very top of the house, it was a long trek up from the kitchen down in the basement.

At mealtimes in the servants' hall nobody was allowed to speak. One can imagine the deathly silence during these meals, with the butler at the head of the table, and the cook down at the opposite end keeping her beady eye on them all of the time. It must have been very unnerving for the young maids. After a rook shoot, it was the girls' job to pluck and feather the dozens of birds ready for the making of rook pies. What a slow and laborious job that must have been. But the rook pies were said to be delicious. I doubt if the rooks would agree.

One morning as Granny was making up the fire, the draught from the big old chimney pulled her apron against the grating of the fire, setting it all alight. She ran out into the passage in fright, where the footman had the presence of mind to catch her, taking a blanket from a side room and rolling her into it quickly on the floor, thereby saving her from terrible burns.

On their rare times off, the girls would sometimes go into Exeter, returning back to the house on the pony and trap, after the driver had dropped their employers off at the station with their luggage. On the rides back to the house, the poor horse made a lot of rude noises with the strain of pulling his load, sending the young girls into fits of giggles, with that, the driver said, 'Oh that is nothing, wait until we go up the hill, he will —— you a whole set of the quadrilles.'

These short outings to Exeter, and the homeward journeys on the pony and trap, must have been a moment of comic relief for those young maids, away from the drudgery of their lives up in the house.

At one time, Granny was in service up in London. It was while she was working there that she queued up with some friends one day, hoping to go on a day trip to Sheerness on the pleasure steamer called *The Princess Alice*. They were very disappointed when they could not get on board, as it was already so crowded. Later the news came through that *The Princess Alice* had been sunk with the loss of 700 lives. So they were very fortunate when they could not find a place on that steamer. It was one of the worst tragedies of the time; many of those lost were little children. This tragedy which Granny was so very nearly in was brought closer to my thoughts with the loss of the ferry the *Herald of Free Enterprise* at Zeebrugge.

While Granny was in service, Grandfather was working at Radley College near Oxford as a dormitory man. This was before he and Grandmother started their courting days, back in their home town of Abingdon. I do not know at what stage in their lives they made their move to Crowthorne, both later working at Wellington College. Records show that Grandad appears to have started working at Wellington in 1882. His brother Albert also made the move to Crowthorne, and his daughter Gladys was to be my mother's little playmate in the years that followed. The brothers' two sisters never married, Lydia dying at an early age and Emily remaining a spinster throughout her life. It was their aunt Emily who was to feature prominently in the children's lives, with their many holidays spent at her little cottage in West St Helens Street in Abingdon. There were many summer picnics spent by the riverside in this pretty little town. Aunt Emily's cottage only had the one bedroom upstairs, and the one living room downstairs, with a tiny scullery on the back, with just an earthenware sink in. Nothing like the standard of kitchens that housewives expect today. There were two toilets up the backyard, which had to serve the three cottages. The children nicknamed them the 'dubs'.

On the picnics by the river, old Aunt Emily was often alarmed by the children's antics of daring to step further and further out into the river while paddling. her shouts to Winnie and Gladie to come back here fell on deaf little ears.

The cottage being close to the church, the children would rush out into the garden as soon as the church bell began to toll. It was a common practice in those days to toll the church bell for the dead: one toll for a child, two tolls for a woman, and three tolls for a man. This was followed by a toll of each year of the deceased person's age. It must have gone on for a very long time if the person was in their eighties.

Opposite Aunt Emily's cottage was the clothing factory. Many of the local women worked there. The children would watch these poor women hurrying to work in the mornings, the latecomers running down the road, only to have the gates shut in their faces as they arrived. They couldn't earn any money that day.

The local baker was a favourite with the little girls. Not only did he have a wide range of goodies for sale through the week, but also on Sundays when he had finished baking his bread, the locals would use his hot oven to put in their roast meat and potatoes for their Sunday lunches. When they were cooked, the baker would walk around the streets, ringing a bell, with people's Sunday roasts on a large platter on his head. The children would wait for him to come around their road, and as soon as they heard his ringing bell, they rushed indoors to let Aunt Emily know that their dinner had arrived.

Aunt Emily was getting on in years when her little nieces came to stay. The old lady would often nod off in her chair in the afternoons, probably worn out with her little charges. One day when the children found her asleep in her chair, they crept out into the scullery, silently collecting all the saucepan lids they could find, then tossing them into the room with such a clatter as to wake the old lady up with a start. They thought it such fun, but these tricks must have almost given my

52

poor great-aunt heart failure. She must have forgiven Winnie and Gladys's little pranks, as their holidays at Aunt Emily's continued throughout most of their childhood, with Emily returning with them for a month's stay in Crowthorne with her brothers and their families. She probably needed that month's break to get over the trauma of the children's fortnight spent in her cottage. In her old age Emily moved into an almshouse in Abingdon which was even smaller than her cottage in St Helens Street. These almshouses can still be seen in Abingdon.

Auntie Emily is still remembered with great affection by my mother, who is now in her eighties. Emily gave them wonderful childhood memories to look back on, of lazy summer days spent paddling in the river and picnicking under the trees, wearing large sun bonnets as protection in the hot sun of years gone past. Also counting the bell tolls of St Helens, and rushing indoors to give their aunt the news of who had died, man, woman or child, and their age. And waiting for the baker with the large platter on his head, containing their ready-cooked Sunday dinner.

Their return to Crowthorne must have seemed a little dull afterwards, with no river to paddle in, and obviously no pranks against Aunt Emily allowed once they were back home again under their parents' control. But there were the lovely pine woods to play in, where children gathered rows and rows of pine needles, making their make-believe houses, to play in while carefully avoiding the large wood-ant hills. If these were disrupted in any way, they would suddenly erupt into a seething black mass of activity, especially if naughty boys poked them with a stick.

When Mother was a toddler, she was given a pretty china teaset as a present. Her little friend Freddie was given a new little hammer. They had a wonderful game as Winnie handed Freddie each piece of china for him to smash, saying 'here's another one, Freddie.' By the time that Granny came out and caught them, the whole new teaset had gone under the hammer.

While the little ones were in Abingdon, their parents would go on a rare trip to the seaside for a break, or maybe a river trip or two. The river trips were very popular in Edwardian days, as old picture postcards show crowded locks of this period. Old Father Thames looked even more crowded than it is today. Boulters Lock was a favourite stopping-off place. Sonning Lock is another pretty place still worth visiting for a peaceful stroll by the riverside. These breaks were short-lived in our grandparents' time, but all the more enjoyable without the din of aircraft noise.

The area around Crowthorne, although beautiful in most parts, had its hidden boggy danger area out towards Owlsmoor. The children were warned never to venture out in that direction. This danger was to be sharply brought home to them one day when a warder from Broadmoor who was new to the district decided to take a short cut to the hospital, only to find himself floundering in the bog, from which there was no escape. His cries for help in the darkness were heard up in the village, and men went forth with lanterns to light their way, as they followed the direction of his pitiful cries. As they picked their way through the darkness, the man's cries, their only means of locating him, became weaker and weaker. When they reached the unfortunate fellow, he was up to his armpits in the bog, and probably would have been dead by morning if his cries for help had gone unheard. After they managed to rescue him, the poor man was in such an exhausted condition he was carried past my grandparent's house up to the hospital to recover from his terrible ordeal

Aunt Emily died before the coming war, so the children's last holiday with her was when the girls were about 13 years old.

When they left school, Mother spent a short period in a draper's shop in Crowthorne High Street which was heated by one of the old-fashioned paraffin heaters. When this old stove was knocked over one day, the owner of the shop had the presence of mind to throw it quickly out into the street; the shop would have been a death trap, as the only entrance was out through the front door. Later both Mother and Aunt Gladys ended up working at Wellington College. Older sister Alice was a milliner in Reading. Winnie loved watching her teenaged sister making the ladies' hats. As a little girl she loved to browse through Alice's sewing room, which was full of silk flowers, ribbons and straw for the hat-making. The little child was often told off by her sister for playing in the sewing room, but Alice made up for her scoldings and would often sit making miniature little hats for Winnie's dolls with the odd scraps of materials which were left over.

When Mother first went to Wellington, she first worked in the Matron's department. One of the most tedious jobs there was the large baskets of boys' socks which all had to be paired up and mended. When the boys were due for a caning, they would dash up to Matron's department first for their thickest pair of pants.

After a period of time, Mother then went to help her parents in the 'Grubbies', the sports and tuck shop for the students, where she was known as Susie to the boys. Very soon she was to meet my father, who came to work there as a trainee cook. They were very young when they started courting, Mother was 15 and Father all of 16. When the First World War came along, Mother's two brothers came back from Canada in army uniforms to fight. Father, being a bit younger, didn't go into the army until it was almost over. Gladys was to lose her brother Victor in the war. Some poor Crowthorne mothers lost as many as four and five sons in the fighting.

Broadmoor at this time had harsh restrictions, no longer practised today. The patients then all wore a white uniform including a white hat. I remember these white outfits still being worn when I was very small, playing in Broadmoor Woods. They certainly stood out, should anyone escape. These restrictions soon disappeared, with modern thinking. As a child I was often taken to see the delightful Broadmoor shows when they were held in the Church House. The patients would travel to different halls in the district by coach. Once Father sat playing cards in the interval with J. Allan, who was called the Mad Parson. This man escaped from Broadmoor in later years and worked as a waiter in London, but was allowed his freedom in the end. It is a pity that one only remembers the names that newspapers dub people with at the time. 'Mad Mitch' also hit the news headlines later. Two of my relatives work in Broadmoor as secretaries, but with the passing of the years there are no longer any members of the Hook family working in Wellington College. Uncle Albert lost his son in the war. After Grandfather's death in 1925, his son Arthur and his wife Edie ran the Grubbies up until 1961.

Mother's brother died of consumption at the early age of 26. Grandfather was in the habit of kissing his dying son goodnight each night, thereby picking up this disease, which was to take his life also. Consumption was the greatest killer at the beginning of this century. Spanish flu was another killer in the First World War. Mother caught it, along with some 450 boys at the college. When she recovered, she had to help nurse the boys, which became a full-time job for the staff for the rest of the term. Next to follow was the awful fire of 1919, which did so much damage to the Orange Dormitory.

My mother arrived late in my grandparents' lives, when they were well into middle age. I have written this little poem, which I think conjures up a picture of their lives at this time.

WINIFRED MAY

Lifetime was hard, in Victorian days,
The labours were long, with so little pay.
But nature repaid, in so many ways,
With sweet family life, in Victorian days.

Their family complete, or so they had thought,
Three sons and a daughter life's riches had brought.
There was Alice and Bill, and Herbert and John,
Their family, they felt, the Lord had smiled on.

The turn of the century came into view,
Schooldays all over, oh how they grew.
Then off to work, before they all knew,
From Father and Mother, a baby was due.

The baby arrived, on a cold wintery day,
A beautiful child they called Winifred May.
Chubby and sweet, her hair all a-curl,
The boys used to spoil this pink baby girl.

She was only but ten when the angels one day
Suddenly came and took Herbert away.
Then came the war, so the boys could not stay.
They were so pleased to have Winifred May.

Lifetime was hard, in post-war days,
The labours were long, with so little pay.
So Canada called, and the boys went away.
They were so pleased to have Winifred May.

Winifred May, the author's mother

56

FAMILY STORIES

Crowthorne village, where my mother grew up with her family, really came into being as a thriving community because of the building of Wellington College and Broadmoor. The flat lands of the college site were excellent for playing fields for the boys, and the sloping nature of the land at Broadmoor was chosen as the high wall surrounding the grounds would not obscure the lovely views from the terrace of the hospital. Most families of the village worked in either of these two places of employment.

Several members of the Hook family worked in different parts of Wellington College. It was my grandparents' job to run the Grubbies, as I mentioned in the last chapter. In later years Uncle Jack and Aunt Edie ran the shop after Grandfather's death. Uncle had spent some time in Canada, before returning to join up for the First World War. One of Grandfather's specialities had been his home-made ice cream, the recipe for which included real strawberries and cream, which was very popular with the boys. King Edward VII,

The Briggs boys opal mining in Australia

The author's uncle in the prairies of Canada

The Squirrel around the turn of the century, when it was owned by George Briggs

while on a visit to the college, asked for a second helping of this iced pudding, as it was named on the menu, so I think that it met with royal approval.

Work was hard to find in England in the early years of this century, and many local young men left to try their luck in Australia and Canada. Life wasn't easy for the Briggs boys, living in a tent, with washing and a tin bath hung out on the bushes. This was life for them in the days before the First World War reared its ugly head, when my father-in-law and his brothers fought with the Anzacs in Gallipoli and in the trenches of France; another brother ended up in Ethiopia. After the war was over, the boys all married, but Alfred was the only one of the brothers to settle permanently in Australia. It was his sons Gordon and Arthur who visited England to see their father's birthplace, The Squirrel. A small class case containing a stuffed red squirrel was still on the wall of the bar, a relic from way back to the 1890s, when George Briggs, their grandfather, lived there.

A lot of Crowthorne lads left to try for work in Canada in the early years of this century, two of my uncles being amongst them. The war also disrupted their lives, and they returned. Uncle Bill ended up in France. After the birth of three more children in England, they returned to Wilkie, Saskatchewan, where they lived out their lives. Their daughter Biddy returned for a visit to England in 1968 to see her old birthplace in Crowthorne, and her husband Don visited places he was stationed at during the Second World War.

Uncle Jack didn't return to Canada after the war, but took Grandfather's place running the Grubbies at Wellington, along with my aunt, until their retirement in the year 1961. They were known as 'Nellie and Arthur' to the boys.

Uncle Frank worked at Wellington College for nearly 40 years. Uncle was a tall, well-built man, who had to endure the discomfort of an artificial limb for most of his life. But he never complained. We children thought of him as the Gentle Giant.

BRACKNELL NEWS

College figure

A porter at Wellington College for 39 years, and known to generations of Old Wellingtonians, Frank Price died in hospital in Reading last week at the age of 81.

Mr Price (he was Mr Francis Price) lived at 53 Wellington Road, Crowthorne. He joined the Grenadier Guards in 1910, becoming a sergeant, but his military career ended in the First World War when he lost a leg in the Battle of Loos in 1916.

He went to Wellington as assistant porter in 1920, later succeeding his father-in-law, Albert Hook, as head porter, and retiring in 1959, the year of the College centenary.

During those celebrations he was presented to the Queen, and he was also presented to the Queen Mother when she visited Wellington to unveil the chapel's stained glass windows in 1952, when our picture was taken.

The author's uncle, Frank Price, meeting the Queen Mother at Wellington College in 1952

60

In 1951 the spire of Holy Trinity was the highest structure in Bracknell...

...Now it is dwarfed by modern office blocks

The public footpath to Easthampstead Church, 1900

The same view today

Church Road at the turn of the century . . .

. . . And a hundred years later

63

Victoria Road, with Victoria Hall, venue for plays and dances

Victoria Hall's replacement

Victoria Road being demolished in 1966

This office block was built 22 years later

Upper Church Road in 1930

It is now a dual carriageway leading to a busy roundabout

The Hind's Head, haunt of highwaymen, at the old crossroads

Bracknell College now stands on the site of the old inn

67

On another corner of the old crossroads was a blacksmith's shop. In this 1915 picture of the High Street it has been replaced by the Forest Hotel, with Dr Fielden's magnificent clock just visible above the carriage.

The Fielden Clock in its new setting in a modern tower

American GIs marching the High Street...

...Which disappeared under this ring road flyover

Queen Victoria changing horses outside the Red Lion...

...Which still survives, in changed surroundings

The Bull in the High Street in 1900, where Henry VIII watched bull-baiting centuries earlier

The Bull today

The old Bullbrook Bridge in London Road

A garage now stands where Taylors Nursery and Water Gardens used to be. The woman is walking where the bridge once was

London Road and Vicarage Lane at the beginning of the century

The same scene 90 years later

Coopers Hill in 1940. The copse on the left is now a subway

Fifty years on, the Bagshot Road has become a dual carriageway

Allsmoor in 1966, home of barn owls and grasshoppers

A supermarket and car park have replaced the field

The Council Offices (later the Labour Exchange) in Rochdale Road

Rochdale Road vanished under this part of Charles Square. Along with the Labour Exchange, the British Legion Hall, the Church House and St John's Hall were demolished

Mill Pond in the 1950s

Today's scene

GHOSTS OF THE NEIGHBOURHOOD

The first haunting that I heard of was near to our home off Church Road, in Kells House just around the corner. Many occupants who had lived in this house felt that it was haunted, some saying it was the ghost of a monk. Visitors have also had the experience of someone brushing past them in the passageway of this house and heard the swishing sound of a robe as it passed by, although nothing could be seen. If this haunting is still occurring today, the phantom will find himself in the middle of a dual carriageway, as Kells House was demolished along with other houses to make way for this road.

Not far from Kells House in Church Road there were two cottages opposite the church, one of which was occupied by an old gentleman who was a friend of ours, and used to come and join us every Sunday for lunch and tea, as Mother felt that he must be lonely after living many years as a widower. He was a very smart old gentleman whose

Kells House in Church Road was reputedly haunted

shoes were so highly polished that we children could see our faces in the shiny toecaps. Next door in the other house lived an old lady. After both old people had passed on, new occupants moved in. But after a short while, one of the new families living there found it quite a disturbing experience as they felt that the house was haunted. They were so alarmed that they sought the help of one of our priests. There didn't seem to be anything of this nature happening there when Father was helping the old gentleman's son in clearing his belongings from the house after his death. I do remember that the house was very dark and gloomy, but dark wallpapers were the fashion when I was a child.

Just across the road at the top of the High Street stood a chemist's shop and estate agent's. Beside the shop was a doorway which led from Church Road and upstairs to rooms over these shops which were used by a tailor and by dental mechanics. It was a common practice for these men to work late into the night when they were busy. Often when we went to bed, we could still see the lights burning in these rooms. But their late working sessions were disturbed by the sound of loud footsteps coming up the stairs from the door which led out into the Church Road. On investigation, nobody could be

So were the rooms over the chemist's shop in the High Street

found. The footsteps were heard on several occasions, always coming up the stairs, never returning back down again. This so unnerved one of the mechanics that he refused to work there after midnight again, as it was always after this hour that their nocturnal visitor came to call.

Many people who experience these strange happenings are afraid to talk about them for fear of being thought 'potty' or given to imagining things, but the other mechanic who worked on alone in the room told my husband that when he heard the familiar footsteps approaching his room yet again, he was afraid to turn around from his bench for fear of actually seeing something.

Bracknell seems to have had its fair share of ghosts, like any other town. And they are not all old tales, as some people would believe. The ghosts of young road accident victims have been seen by later occupants of their old homes.

Surprisingly, despite its evil past, the Hinds Head seems to have been free of ghosts. Not so the Old manor, which has had ghostly inhabitants through the years, the most persistent being that of a lady up in one of the bedrooms.

A recent haunting happened in one of the local shops. A man carrying parcels was seen approaching the back of the shop across the car park, watched by some of the staff who were having a tea break. One of them opened the door to let him in but, in full view of everyone there, he disappeared through the wall. This gave everyone a shock, to say the least, and they went up to the police station with their story. One of the policemen seemed quite used to hearing ghost stories. He got out an old map of the area and pinpointed a lane on the old map which, if it were still in use, would lead straight to where the man disappeared. After this first sighting the ghost started appearing quite frequently, so that the staff began to get used to his presence. When I asked my friend what he looked like, she described him as a little man, wearing a smock coat, rather like the ones worn by farmers etc. at the turn of the century. On entering the stockroom one day and encountering the apparition there, she decided not to tell the others, so when one of the other ladies went into the room a few moments later, and quickly emerged saying, 'He is in there again', my friend was satisfied that it wasn't all due to her imagination. She began to sense when he was there, even if she couldn't see him in her part of the shop, as the atmosphere turned cold with his arrival. One day when they arrived for work, they could see the apparition in the window; also things started disappearing from the shop premises. After a thorough search was made, and the missing items could not be found, replacements were sent for. When these arrived, the original items would mysteriously reappear from nowhere. About this time there was a change of management at the shop, and when a customer made a remark about the cold atmosphere of the place, it was decided that the help of a priest was needed. Since that time the little man has been seen no more.

Visual ghosts have been seen in other parts of Bracknell, in South Hill Park, and at Easthampstead Park, but they have all been well documented in other books of the area, so I will not repeat them all over again. These are just the strange experiences of friends and relatives, so we know that they are true statements of what happened.

There are many ghost horses around the district that are heard and not seen. While the workmen were pulling down the old Royal Ascot Hotel they said they often heard the neighing of a horse in the empty building and the stamping of feet. Ghost horses are still heard around the area of Kennel Lane in Bracknell. Some friends who live in a cottage that is a converted stable have also had this experience, and often hear strange sounds in the bedrooms which were originally the hayloft.

I never used to believe a ghost story we were told at school of a horse in Ralphs Ride which could be heard galloping along, but could not be seen. We jokingly called him 'Ralph' on his horse, for want of a better name. If any children misbehaved, we would say, 'Ralph will get you on his horse.' On growing up, this silly childhood spook story went completely out of my mind until twenty years later we had a strange experience shortly after moving house. As we sat watching television one dark evening, we heard a loud sound of a horse gallop past the window. It was so heavy that it shook the room as it passed. We all looked at each other, wondering what to do. The children sat open-mouthed, waiting for an explanation. Quickly taking a torch, we ventured around the garden, with the children watching from the safety of the porch. We thought its hooves must have ruined the lawn, remembering the damage done by straying farm animals on market days. Not really knowing how we would calm the frightened animal, as neither of us is very good with horses at close quarters, we stealthily crept around the garden, and were somewhat relieved to find nothing there. But we were even more puzzled in the morning light to find no evidence of our nocturnal visitor. As we searched the night before, we truly felt that the vandals had turned Joe Brant's pony loose again, which often happened. (This did sadly happen on a later date, and Joe's pony was killed in Bracknell one evening after these vandals let it loose for the last time.)

About five years later I was talking to a neighbour of Mother's, when the conversation got around to the fact that Lily Hill House was haunted, and she asked me in to look at some lovely old pictures that she had kept of the house, which were taken when she was a young chambermaid there, along with her sister. While looking at the pictures and talking about the strange things that happened in the house, I mentioned the evening about our non-existent horse. She laughed and said, 'Oh, that will only be old Dick on his horse. He has often been heard by locals up your way, as his ghost still jumps the toll gate, and then he is heard to gallop up over the Links.' I found her stories very interesting, while at the same time taking them with a pinch of salt. But this changed when I returned home and had time to ponder her story. I realised that the Links used to be where we are now living – Links Cottage is only a few doors away, and the toll gate was just up the road near Toll Cottage. If the rider and his horse jumped the toll gate and then galloped up over the Links, they would end up in Ralphs Ride, so the spook story told to us in the playground seems to be the same phantom as that of Dick Turpin on Lily Hill. I don't know if there was a toll gate there in Turpin's time; the phantom could be that of another highwayman. We did not hear him again, but we didn't think to take note of the date and time either.

This lady was also able to throw some light on an experience that my brother-in-law had while working alone in Lily Hill House. As he was working he became aware of doors opening and shutting all over the house. He went to investigate, in case someone had come from the builder's yard and was looking for him. But as he walked over the house, all was quiet, and finding himself the only occupant, he went back to work. After a short time he heard the sound of doors opening and shutting as before. At first he took no notice and carried on with his work, but gradually the continual opening and closing of the doors in other parts of the house began to make him feel uneasy, and he was wishing his work was finished so that he could leave. By the time that the job was done, the eerie echoing sound of the banging doors were really getting to him, and he rather hastily gathered up all of his tools and left. The lady replied, 'Oh my goodness. Is that still happening after all these years? That used to happen to us when we were maids fifty years ago. We would go into a room to draw the curtains, only to find the door locked when we came to go out again. It was always happening, after entering a room the door would close behind us for no apparent reason.' In fact it happened so often that their father, who also worked there, would have to come to the windows with a ladder, and let the girls out. My bother-in-law's experience was about 15 years ago now, but as I take a stroll in Lily Hill Park and look at the house, I often wonder if the doors are still opening and shutting by themselves.

As a teenager I used to go cycling with friends to many of the local ponds dotted about the area. Dry Pond on the Crowthorne Road was a favourite spot to relax by on a summer's day. There wasn't the heavy traffic using the road in the 1950s, so it was a peaceful place compared to today. Incidentally the pond was never dry, to live up to its name, although the water level did drop during the summer months. Another favourite ride was to Gormoor Pond, where my giggling friends and I used to sit and sun ourselves on its banks. But by far the easiest to get to was Mill Pond, which had to be visited on foot, due to its isolated location, and to the fact that two, maybe three stiles had to be negotiated on the way. The modern facelift of the pond makes it look very different today from its natural beauty of years ago. But the old pond is still giving pleasure and recreation to a lot of people. The pond used to be surrounded by thick woodland in parts. If approached from St Michaels end of Mill Lane, stiles had to be climbed over first, and also the mill stream had to be negotiated by means of a fallen tree which acted like a bridge to cross over. This was a favourite haunt of courting couples. After emerging from the woods, another stile had to be climbed over to reach the pool. It was always a very silent place. This was part of its charm; one's footsteps breaking the dried-up twigs in the undergrowth were an intrusion into the silent brooding atmosphere of the pond and its surroundings. If one sat quietly on its banks, the only sound to be heard was the whistling murmur of the breeze disturbing the reeds and rushes which grew all around the pools shoreline. One might suddenly be startled by the screech of a waterfowl flying up from its nest hidden amongst the reeds on the waters edge, but this uneasiness was short-lived as one wondered what had disturbed the bird, and the silence descended all around once more.

It was a surprise therefore to read a story in a recent newspaper that the mill was haunted. Which is just as well we didn't know, as this knowledge might have spoilt the many carefree hours spent there in the past. The story goes that during the seventeenth century a miserly farmer lived in a mill which stood by the pond. One harsh winter's day the farmer slammed the door on a man who was begging for food. The next morning the farmer found him frozen to death on the doorstep. From then on the farmer and his family were plagued with bad luck. The cattle began to die, his land flooded and his crop failed. The family were haunted by the man's ghost, and became very poor, so that eventually they had to flee the mill. For years the locals would not go near, and the mill became a ruin. Finally a brave band of villagers set fire to the mill, purging the area of its symbol of terror. I do not know if this tale is true. There was a mill house standing there after in 1815, as the old print shows, but maybe it replaced the one that was fired.

Not all hauntings are unhappy affairs, as a newspaper story appeared about an old house in Broad Lane where the ghosts of happy laughing children were often heard running up the stairs in the house, but when the owner went to investigate where they had gone and all the bedrooms were found to be silent and empty.

But the presence in a house up on Rounds Hill in Bracknell felt malevolently disposed to visitors when we went to view the house in the late 1960s, when our own house was due to be compulsorily purchased. We had to find somewhere else fairly quickly, as the developers were pressing us to get out. But this was a house that I just could not consider moving into. On entering the hall all seemed quite normal, except that the property needed an awful lot of alterations carried out on it to bring it up to the standard of our nicely decorated home in Rochdale Road. The two downstairs front rooms were not too bad, but on entering the kitchen, it all smelt very musty and dark. Three large pipes ran straight up in front of the window, which was very strange, so they would have to be removed and plumbed in elsewhere. The floor of the kitchen had a curious sunken part in the middle, which would have meant more work to level out.

By this time the others had gone upstairs to view the bedrooms. I was alone downstairs as I wandered back out into the hall that we first entered on our arrival. For some curious reason I felt uneasy, and the hall had felt strangely cold too when we first arrived. I had the feeling of being watched, and as I started to climb the stairs I felt a tap on my shoulder which sent a shiver down my spine. It was a touch similar to when a person behind wishes to speak to you, but when I turned around the hall was empty. A sense of foreboding came over me as I climbed the stairs, still feeling a presence following behind. I told myself not to be so stupid, here was I, a grown woman, acting like a frightened child.

On joining the others I felt a little better, and began to scold myself for being so silly. I looked at the bedrooms, which weren't too bad, a papering job would soon make them look a lot better; but I couldn't shake off feeling cold although it was a summer's day. John then told me to go and look at the bathroom, which he said needed a lot doing to it. When I peered into the bathroom it was pitch-black, as there wasn't a window and the electricity was turned off. I could see that it was a largish room, rather like a bedroom that had been made into a bathroom. I could just make out an old bath in the corner through the gloom, when I had the sensation of someone looking over my shoulder, and a cold atmosphere started to envelop me as before. I turned to call the others, but found they were now outside in the garden. On finding myself alone once more, I didn't hesitate this time and fled downstairs and out into the garden. It was such a relief to get outside, where everything became so warm and normal, with the birds singing and the noise of the traffic passing on the busy road outside. Sounds which were so welcome after the oppressive foreboding atmosphere of that house. My husband and brother-in-law were discussing how much land there was to build an extension on the side of the property, when I said flatly that I didn't want to live there. I just knew that I couldn't go inside that house again, but didn't want to say that I felt it was haunted – it would seem silly to them.

I had never felt like that in any of the other houses we had looked at in previous weeks of searching. But sometime later, we met some friends who we found out had also viewed the house. I asked as casually as I could what they thought of the place, when the wife answered quickly, saying how awful she thought it was, and so creepy! Especially the hall and stairs. For some curious reason I felt so much better after meeting them. Needless to say they did not purchase the house either.

Since a graveyard was dug up in the Old High Street and a banking court built where the church used to be, many girls who work in the banks have said that they feel that the vaults are now haunted, but by a benevolent presence, not a malevolent one.

During 1992–3, a lady appeared in the vicinity of Kennel Lane School. The Kennel Lane area has a history of ghostly sounds of horse-drawn coaches pulling to a halt, but on investigation by people living in this neighbourhood, nothing can be seen to account for these sounds.

The lady in grey was first noticed by a local woman who worked at the school. This apparition was dressed in a beautiful dove-grey riding habit, the coat of which had tiny small buttons all up the front. A long riding skirt fell over the top of high-buttoned boots of yesteryear, the kind that needed a special hook to fasten its many buttons. For some reason the witness felt that the boots were not the right kind for riding.

The beautiful apparition had lovely golden hair tucked up under her riding hat, and seemed to be looking for something or someone.

The observer's first reaction was to ask the horsewoman if she needed help, as she looked lost in some way. But something made her study the figure more closely before speaking; something was strange and not quite right. The realisation came to her that she was observing a person attired in clothing not worn in the 1990s.

The figure of this rider lingered for quite a while, and appeared on several later occasions, but gradually becoming more indistinct with each following sighting. Several local people have been studying old history books to try and find out who she was and what may have happened to her, causing her to linger in this melancholy way in Kennel lane. Maybe a riding accident in the past in which the rider or her horse died?

The witness of this beautiful apparition always had the feeling that the lady was looking for her horse. Who could she have been?

The next story is not a ghost story, but about a sad and strange tombstone in the middle of a road junction.

When I was a child, the junction at the east end of Park Road was not as it appears today. In olden days, there was a triangular-shaped piece of land fenced off in the middle of the road. Traffic going to Warfield went to the left of the triangle, while traffic for Bracknell kept to the other side. Bay Road and Holly Spring Lane crossed from south to north in front of the triangle. On the side of Holly Spring lane was the well by Sheppe's Farm. Some recent books state that it had healing powers, a holy well, but I have never heard this from any of the old locals. It was just a well, from which Holly Spring Lane acquired its name.

There was another well situated in the triangle on the road junction. Just inside the fence was a very old tombstone. Apparently, a lady had the misfortune to fall down this well and was drowned. Villagers were unable to retrieve her body, so a tombstone was erected above the well to the memory of this unfortunate lady. A friend of mine, Alice Matthews, used to stop and look at this sad stone as a child, while on her way to collect milk for her mother from Sheppe's Farm. But unfortunately she cannot remember the name on this stone, only that the Christian name was Louisa; but the surname is forgotten.

There is another sad little story concerning a pond which was in the grounds of Warfield Park. The mansion was demolished long ago, but the pond remains. A young girl by the name of Rachel drowned in the pond years ago. It still retains a melancholy atmosphere, and is now known as Rachel's Pond. Nobody seems to know if Rachel was a member of the family who owned Warfield Park, or if Rachel was a servant girl.

The next ghost story is recalled for us in all of its vivid detail by an old Bracknell resident who now lives in South Penrith, New South Wales. Although Mr James has lived in Australia for 34 years, and during the war he survived Dunkirk, the Middle East and Malaya, it is his experience of his unusual encounter with an apparition in Bracknell as a child that has stayed fresh in his memory, although it happened so many years ago. Unfortunately the pond and the surrounding area of this story has been buried under the development of the New Town.

The story starts with Frank and his sister Phyllis, who was 12 at the time, being sent on an errand for their mother to a shop in Binfield Road. In order to reach the shop, the children had to cross some allotments and a plank over a stream during this journey. They carried with them a home-made lantern comprising of a candle stuck into the bottom of a large jam jar, as darkness had already fallen.

The pond was situated in the far right-hand corner of the allotment, replenished by a small stream running directly across Bull Lane. The lane ran alongside and beyond the Bull Inn, which was famous for its bull-baiting in days of old. Henry VIII often visited Bracknell for this barbaric sport.

The pond interior was always dark and foreboding, giving it an eerie look as it was surrounded by thick masses of blackberry bushes. The front of the pond was open, but overgrown with reeds. There still remained remnants of a wooden fence, although completely covered over by bushes, suggesting in the past that the pond was used as a watering hole for cattle etc. Frank says, 'We had crossed over the stream by way of the plank, when we were stopped dead in our tracks by the sudden appearance of a large black horse being led out of the blackness of the pond by a young man, who seemed to be having difficulty handling the high-spirited animal. The horse was whinnying and nodding its head, then stopped and began stamping the ground with its two front hooves. The young rider, however, commenced patting the horse and speaking to it in low tones, which appeared to have little success, then after making some adjustment to the reins, the young man climbed into the saddle and rode away into the night, following the stream in the direction of Bull Lane.

'All of this happened in a few seconds, and our first reaction was to drop the jam jar and scramble back over the plank, screaming and falling over each other in the process. Eventually, having reached home in our hasty retreat, we both tried to explain to our mother what we had just witnessed in a gibberish fashion, which apparently must have given her some indication that there was a reason for our strange behaviour. Whether or not she believed the story we told, I don't really know to this day, because it was never mentioned again, and we were never sent on any more errands after dark.

'Looking back over this rather disturbing event, I am inclined to believe that it was neither the horse or the man coming out of the pond that really frightened us, but the fact that we were seeing something that should not have been there.

'The horse in question was a magnificent animal, being black in colour and heavily proportioned, similar to the ones used in heavy work like ploughing or hauling timber. It certainly was not the type of mount one would normally see being used for the pleasure of horse riding. I can remember seeing small chain-mail armour on the horse's head, reaching down along the neck and also across its back between tail and saddle. The tail of the horse was neatly interlaced, which indicated the animal was well cared for.

'There is not very much that I can tell you about the young rider, except that he was of medieval style, with stockinged legs, and he also wore small chain-mail armour reaching down from shoulder to the waistline. I did not see his face because he had his back to us while attending to his horse. There was no sign of any weapon of any description, which would have been expected due to the fact that with the display of chain-mail armour, one could form the conclusion that both man and horse were prepared for combat.

'The following morning my sister and I stopped and inspected the area in front of the pond on our way to school, hoping to find some evidence of our nocturnal visitor, such as hoof prints etc. There was absolutely nothing to suggest that a horse had been there the night before, but the jam jar was still there where my sister had dropped it when we made our hurried departure, and that was all.'

We haven't been able to trace any other witnesses of the apparition of Bull Lane, of the young rider and his black horse, who may have later died in combat. Who knows!

I was told the next story by a local postman, who while on his rounds had made friends with two workmen whose job it was to demolish each property up in Ralph's Ride as it became vacant. An old stray dog began to stay with them and slept with them as they moved from place to place. This night they had decided to sleep in one of the bungalows, while they pulled down the others in the vicinity. After taking in their bedding etc. they settled down with the old dog for the night. They were disturbed sometime later by someone walking about in the next room. On entering this room, they found it to be empty. The men also checked around the outside of the property for prowlers. On finding no one they went back inside to settle down once more.

After a while, the footsteps were again heard coming from the adjoining room, and the old dog was becoming agitated. This time they went to investigate. On entering the room they sent the dog in first, whose hair immediately stood up along its back, its ears dropped and its tail went down between its legs in fright. It bolted back out past the two men and off into the woods, and they never saw it again.

They again checked all around the outside of the building, but couldn't find anyone or anything that would account for the dog's strange behaviour, so decided to settle down for some well-earned sleep. As they lay there discussing the dog and the footsteps, an old mangle, which was rusty with age and had obviously been standing in the corner for years, suddenly started to move! As the alarmed men watched, the heavy old mangle hurtled across the floor, hitting the opposite wall with such a force that it almost went through. With this, they decided that enough was enough, and hastily gathered up their belongings and left. They said that in all of their years of travelling the countryside doing demolition jobs, they had never come across anything as strange as this.

The ghost of 50 Berkeley Square in London is a famous tale appearing in many books. But one story involved a Bracknell resident, one Sir Robert Warboys, the 7th Baronet, a young man of just turned 30, whose country seat was supposed to have been a large Queen Anne House at Bracknell in Berkshire. The strange thing about this story is that after searching through Bracknell Library with the Librarian's help, we could not find any information on the existence of Sir Robert, or of where his country seat was in Bracknell, but his gruesome death was caused by an encounter with the ghost of Berkeley Square, as was the death of a sailor who later was foolish enough to enter the haunted room of No. 50.

As there is only one Bracknell in England, indeed the world, it seems strange that we cannot trace Sir Robert. Perhaps a reader can, but I do not know if Sir Robert is fact or fiction. Maybe he is just that, 'a story'.

Windsor Forest, which used to spread beyond Bracknell, has many ghosts, one of which was encountered by John's uncle during the war, while he was a special policeman. Arthur didn't take too much notice of a man near the vicinity of Hernes Oak, until he vanished into thin air, but he never forgot it.

The most famous phantom is that of Herne the Hunter, who dressed in deerskins and his helmet of a stag's scull and antlers. He must be a fearsome sight. The old Hernes Oak was destroyed in 1863, but the spectral hunter and his pack have been seen quite recently in the Long Walk. Henry VIII was twice to encounter the ghost of Herne the Hunter, once in the forest, and once on the battlements of the castle. George III is the most persistent ghost at the castle, closely followed by that of the spectre of Elizabeth I.

The vicinity of Dry Pond was reputed to be haunted years ago by the ghost of a man who hanged himself from one of the oak trees nearby. Many years later a horse became so uneasy as it approached the pond that on reaching it he refused to move. The owner of the horse and cart became impatient and urged the horse on with a strike of his whip. With this, the horse bolted past the pond, and could not be pulled up again for many miles.

No doubt other locals have many more stories of the ghosts in our district; these are but just a few of the phantoms of Bracknell. If you should be in the right place, at the right time, and encounter one, it's an experience you will never forget!

LIFE IN THE OLD DAYS

House mice were a pest years ago, and could only be caught properly in the old spring traps. We were lucky enough never to have these persistent little invaders in our pantry, but now and again a mouse would find its way into the bedroom cupboard over the stairs. A trap was always left set in this cupboard ready for any little visitors. I hated to hear it go off, as the trap would often bounce around on the floor for a few seconds after the mouse was caught. Thank goodness that mice do not invade houses as they used to do.

The old toilets years ago were often handy hiding places for rats and mice, being boxed-in, square-shaped structures, often in sheds at the bottom of the garden. We were lucky in that we had a toilet joined onto the back of the house, but one still had to go outside to it, and as the other half was the coal shed, we often heard the scuffle of mice, especially after dark, when a candle had to be taken with you to light the way. Mother was frightened of mice, so she told us to knock the boxed toilet with our feet, and this would frighten any mice away, should they be lurking there. We always knew when the little room was in use, as loud knocking noises came from that direction.

Father was told a tale by a farmer friend of his who had had the misfortune to be bitten by a rat, in a rather private place, while in his toilet. he said, 'He was a beauty, I had to take him to the doctor.' I wonder if the doctor managed to keep a straight face while treating this patient.

When harvesting and haymaking time came around in our grandparents' time, everyone was expected to help out. Even the children were taken along as their mothers worked hard in the fields. The large hats and long dresses must have been a hindrance for women – not exactly suitable attire for working in hot summmers.

The lovely sound of the grasshoppers are rarely heard in Bracknell now. It was lovely to sit in the old Cricket Field and hear the strange singing sound of the grasshoppers on a lovely warm day.

A familiar sight in homes in the old days, which I, for one, was very pleased to see the end of, was the use of sticky fly-papers. To see dozens of dying flies stuck on these papers was just too much for a little girl's stomach. Also the practice of putting out jam jars full of fruit juice, with a hole in the lids to catch unwary wasps, was one that my sisters and I couldn't stand. Often while out of sight of our

Ladies helping with haymaking, 1900

parents, we would operate little rescue missions by poking a stick through the hole and allowing the insects to crawl up it and escape. If we were caught doing this, the menfolk would come and swish the jar all around in front of our horrified little eyes. We also disliked the cruelty dealt out by boys with their catapults, but this was nothing compared to today's cruelty with the use of guns and crossbows on our unsuspecting wild creatures.

One of my earliest recollections is taking father his lunchbox to the egg packing station and being allowed to watch for a while as the eggs went along on a machine that resembled a little train, being stamped in the process, then rolling down into different grading trays. I used to watch spellbound from my pushchair, waiting for the eggs to break under this rough treatment, but few ever did. In later years eggs were to be stamped with little lions on them, supposedly proving their freshness, but some of the eggs that we used to get smelt awful when cracked open. The little lion sign had done nothing to prove freshness, and one still had to rely on one's nose for this purpose. Little were we to know that in the coming war years, these useful little items would be rationed and we would have to rely on the powdered kind instead.

Before the shortage, I remember buckets of eggs being preserved in our larder, and how we used to love diving our hands into the slimy mixture of water-glass to retrieve some eggs for Mum's cooking sessions.

Between the wars it was back to work. International Stores staff in the early 1930s...

...And play. Ascot races around the same time

In 1937 Bracknell celebrated the Coronation with a beauty contest

The Warfield Coronation procession

Long before the closure of the egg packing station, many other businesses had failed to prosper, including several brickfields, the brewery and basket making – the osier beds were situated in Rochdale Road – and Lawrences Stores closed its doors. The timber merchants followed and Rainbow Fireworks later disappeared from Bracknell. Sandwith's Crayon Factory carried on until its premises were demolished to make way for a roundabout. The firm moved to Wimborne in Dorset, taking several employees with them.

Back in 1937, Bracknell was a thriving market town and a close-knit community. So when the Coronation of George VI and Queen Elizabeth was announced for 12th May, Bracknell and its surrounding villages celebrated the day in great style with parties, bathing beauty contests, carnival floats and processions around the decorated streets.

The costumes for Coronation Day were splendid medieval affairs. One of the attendants lost her job for entering the beauty contest, an occasion frowned on by some of the local gentry. But the Marchioness of Downshire entered into the spirit of the celebrations by crowning the Queen, even if a little crookedly, an event which still seems to happen in the 'Miss World' contests today.

The winner, the Coronation Queen, and her attendants in medieval dress

95

THE EVACUEES

They came bewildered, confused and afraid,
At home with their families, they would rather have stayed.
But Hitler's cruel bombs were all around,
A quick and safe refuge had to be found.

For the little ones, it was a time of fear,
To have to leave, and not have Mother near.
Why must they go, from homes that they know?
Into the midst of strangers they had to go.

As trains bore them forth to the countryside,
From Hitler's harsh blitz they came to hide.
Into strange schools, and into strange homes,
Came the bewildered, little innocent ones.

Onto the platform, to have their name checks,
With gasmasks in boxes, around their necks.
Oh! What a trauma, for these little ones' heads.
There were many tears, and many wet beds.

In the Second World War, evacuees in Wokingham included Doris and Renee Baker

As time passed by, flourished friendships new,
With Renee and Doris, and Cynthia we grew.
As war came to a close, they all went away.
Where are you now? I am wondering today.

The airmen called Bill, and Stan, and dear Paul,
Did you survive that cruel war at all?
The Dutch boys who were so sweet and kind,
Where are you now, our wartime friends?

The smart young GIs in their fancy clothes,
To the local girls they gave new nylon hose.
Off as young brides, to a far distant shore,
For some of their folks, to be seen no more.

And Cynthia Nicholson with the author's family

BRACKNELL IN WORLD WAR II

It is hard to imagine now, all these years later, our cramped sleeping arrangements of the war years, but our friends up in London were suffering much greater hardships in the bombing raids than we could ever imagine.

We found our little bunker under the stairs quite exciting, but Bud Ellis, on waking one night, sat up without realising where he was, and cracked his head on the underside of the stairs. We all had to be rearranged to give him more headroom. While all of this was going on, our eldest sister was watching the proceedings from her bed made up under the dining room table. The airmen billeted on us slept on camp beds in the front room downstairs, and in our bedroom. It was like one big happy family. Charlie came from Wales, Stan from Preston, Eddie and Bill were Londoners. Dear Charlie died from the effects of an injury to his jaw, the others we never heard from again.

The Dutch boys used to walk into Bracknell from their camp out in Easthampstead Park. When they turned up on the doorstep of a Sunday afternoon, Mum somehow managed to lay out a nice tea for them from our wartime rations. But very often the fruit cake had liquid paraffin in the recipe, replacing the fat which was often unobtainable.

In the summer months it was easier as salad stuffs were plentiful, every small piece of ground was put to good use for growing vegetables etc, stretching out our meagre rations. Every harvest of apples, plums and greengages was promptly bottled ready for the coming winter months. The raspberries and blackcurrants were quickly made up into jams. There was only a one-pound jar of jam per person during food rationing, and that jar had to last a month. I remember that I always chose apricot for my monthly ration, as this was a jam Mum couldn't make, being a foreign fruit. Bracknell was well endowed with blackberry bushes in those days, so we youngsters spent hours out blackberry picking for our mothers. Acorns were also gathered for the pig farmers. Chestnuts were roasted on our open fires in the autumn. Nothing was left to waste.

Father was very proud of his marrow heap, until a courting couple started using it, flattening his treasured marrows into the ground. A little tripwire was set up for their next nightly jaunt, but when Dad heard a kerfuffle in the darkness the following night, he felt so guilty and removed the wire the next morning, but our marrows were never ruined and squashed into the ground again, so it did the trick.

One day we took a trip up to visit friends in Hounslow, and were fascinated by the Ellises' large steel table, under which beds were made up for a little protection in bombing raids. However, later, the Ellis family were able to move into an empty house in Rochdale Road for the rest of the duration of the war.

Towards the end of this period there was great excitement when their eldest daughter Joan was married in Bracknell to her GI bride-groom Eddie. I remember my disappointment when the bride wasn't dressed all in white. Being just a child, I didn't realise that wartime weddings were often hastily arranged during the couples' leave etc.

GI bride Joan with her husband Eddie

A white gown was often out of the question with the clothing rationing, when coupons had to be put to a more useful purpose in the brides trousseau, which could be used once the wedding day was over.

Families and friends also used to pool their coupons if there was a wedding, in order to collect enough for the ingredients of a modest wedding cake.

Just a small cake for the occasion was all that could be managed, none of the three- and four-tier cakes that are the norm today.

Joan's hairstyle was typical of the forties, with curls piled high on the top of the head, held in with hairpins and left long at the back. Many film stars had this style, which local girls copied at the time. Her tall hat and serviceable woollen suit was also typical of wartime styles. Towards the end of the war, pillbox hats were all the rage, tilted forward at a jaunty angle and decorated with lots of veiling.

But many couples just got married in their wartime uniforms in haste to tie the knot, with the future so uncertain for them at this time.

We children loved the double summertime of the war years, with the very light evenings. Often in the summer when it was too hot to get to sleep, Mum would let us join them in the garden until after the bombers had gone over. We sat in our deckchairs, looking up at the evening sky watching the nightly ritual going on. We had a small lawn between the district nurse's house next door and our own.

High up under the eaves of our house were several pairs of swifts nesting. These little birds came back, year after year. There must have been great confusion for them in later years when our houses were demolished, depriving them of their homes also, after their thousands of miles flight to get here to nest. It was always a joy to hear their familiar squealing call each year on their arrival, as it meant that summer was really here at last. In the late evenings they were at their busiest, whirling around the sky catching insects during wonderful acrobatic aerial displays, and swooping up under the eaves with such precision to feed their young then ending the evening sweeping and squealing about the sky overhead, before finally going in to roost for the night.

The rooks' nightly procession across the evening sky was a more sedate affair. Unhurried and cawing their hoarse-sounding calls to one another, they ambled along in an untidy formation. There were hundreds of these loveable old birds winding their slow progress across the sky going home to roost. Then at last the dawdling few stragglers would appear with much cawing noise as they tried to catch up. The sky seemed strangely quiet as their calls grew fainter in the distance.

Sadly neither of these species are seen much over Bracknell any more, just the odd one or two now and again. I used to think that the swifts were like spitfires of the skies, and rooks like the slow bombers.

When it was almost dark the hedgehogs would trundle noisily out of their daytime sleeping quarters under the thick ferns which grew against the wall. Where the swifts had been noisily squealing a short time before, the silent bats were now swooping about, taking their nightly feed on the evening insects, shortly followed by the eerie hoot of an owl from his lofty perch high up in the poplar tree behind the Boys' Clubhouse.

Then the sound that we had been waiting for could be faintly heard in the distance: the familiar heavy droning sounds of the nighttime bombers approaching, carrying their brave young crews forth on their missions of saving us from Hitler's grasp.

Our house hadn't got a bathroom, so it was quite a scramble in the mornings with everyone taking turns at the kitchen sink, the men shaving, Mother getting us washed ready for school and making sure that we had got our gas masks and lunch boxes. There wasn't electricity down the lane, so all washing water had to be heated on the gas. Mum used to bath us in front of the fire, in an old tin bath, with the clothes horse acting as a screen. I remember my sister being most

Ken Hope from Bracknell (third from left) with his wartime bomber crew

101

indignant because Eddie, one of the airmen, peered at her having a bath behind this makeshift screen, but I was too young to worry about such things.

But I was to be frightened later by a soldier hanging about in the lane while I was playing with our little dog Judy. He made friends with the dog, then beckoned me to follow him up the lane. In my childlike innocence I did so, but when I reached the spot where he was hiding in the bushes, something told me that what he was doing was terribly wrong. He was saying 'Come on, little girl', but there was something very strange in his smile, more of a leer and unfriendly. Luckily I took to my heels and ran back down the lane as fast as my legs could carry me, but the stones of the lane seemed to be impeding my progress, such was the fear that he was chasing me. As I nearly reached our houses, I became aware of the fact that Judy was running close beside me. What worried Mother was the fact that this man was waiting for me in the lane the next day, but I had gone to school. Mother called our neighbour out, and the man emerged out of the bushes, but stayed in Bug Lane a short distance away, hiding behind a wall. Mum went into Brown's builders' yard for assistance, where a lot of local men were working. When she emerged from the yard with Mr Spencer, the soldier came out of his hiding place and ran up to Mount Pleasant like a hare.

Now the seeds of doubt had been planted in my young mind, and everywhere I went afterwards I was expecting him to be hiding somewhere waiting for me. When I did see him in Church Road some time later, luckily there was another soldier with him so I rushed past, looking back to make sure that they weren't following. Both men were turned, laughing at me, and my little legs turned to jelly at that moment. I didn't encounter him in the village after that day, but he was always at the back of my mind.

I'd had my first experience of a flasher at the ripe old age of six. My sisters and I were to encounter other strange men in later years at the recreation ground, where the Met Office now stands. My sister was approached by a man who wanted to take her to the swings. Luckily it was market day, so she was able to run and tell our dad, who was working there. These incidents taught us a lesson in self-preservation.

The skies over Bracknell had their tragic incidents during the war. Two Boston planes collided in front of our house. Mother and I were in her front bedroom when we heard the bang. Looking out of the window, we were horrified to see one plane in a nosedive hurtling down at great speed. It was like watching the other plane in slow motion. The fuselage was falling quite quickly, but one of the wings was still spinning high in the air above it, and we watched in silence

In the Second World War, Minster Street in Reading suffered in a 1943 bombing raid

as it fluttered earthwards like a broken butterfly wing. Mum and I didn't speak for a few moments, but just stood gazing at the empty sky where the two planes had been shortly before, wondering how many men were dying in that moment. My husband was a lad walking home from school at the time. He saw the planes flying side by side; they got too close and collided, snapping off the wings, and both crews were killed. A very sad incident, long remembered by the locals. But boys will be boys, and many a little local lad collected pieces of the plane wreckage, which were scattered all around Harmans Water. A Mosquito plane crashed near Caesar's Camp, and a German Messerschmitt crashed in Easthampstead. One pilot's body was found in the garden of a bungalow in Bagshot Road.

In February 1943 Reading suffered a bad bombing raid. Mum and my sister were going by train to the Palace Theatre, but waited for a later train to make sure that I was home from school first, before leaving me in Dad's care. If they had caught the earlier one, they would have been walking in the vicinity where the bombs dropped. The People's Pantry received a direct hit, killing many people. Wellsteads Store was badly damaged by the hit-and-run raider, and buildings in Minster Street ended up like just heaps of rubble. The local church was also damaged. When Mother and my sister arrived, the raiders were still machine-gunning the streets. ARP personnel and soldiers were searching for victims all night by the light of hurricane lamps. Amongst all of this chaos, the show still carried on at the Palace Theatre, with Wee Georgie Wood as the star. It is funny how people just carried on with what they were doing at these times. Mother didn't think of coming home in case the raiders came back, but still went into the theatre as planned. As it was, the siren alert sounded while they were watching the show, but everyone sat tight.

Back in the year of 1940 Wellington College was hit by two high-explosive bombs and two incendiaries. The Master, Mr Longden, came out of the lodge at the moment a high-explosive bomb fell in the forecourt, and he was killed instantly. The lodge was wrecked, and the library and chapel badly damaged. I remember my uncle Frank showing us the shattered dormitories later, while we were on a visit to our relatives. My auntie Edie was relaxing in her bungalow in the college grounds, when she was shot out of her armchair onto the floor by the blast. Luckily the boys had taken to the shelters. The boys continued to stay in the shelters every night into 1941. An unpopular practice, but necessary in the circumstances.

One night when Dad was ill in bed with the flu, the warden came banging on the door for Father to go out fire-watching. Mother explained that he couldn't join them that night. As she went to the door to let the warden out, she saw that the whole of the sky was lit up like day with flares. Hundreds of incendiaries fell around the woodlands that night, especially in Harmans Water. Luckily none of them found their target of the ammunition dumps hidden under the trees around Bracknell. We would have been in for a nasty surprise if they had gone up.

A barrage balloon used to float in the sky beyond the oak tree behind the Boys Club, but one morning it had broken loose and became a danger to our planes. Mother watched as a plane chased it and shot it down. I was very annoyed at having missed this bit of excitement while I was in school, but I noticed the balloon had gone the minute I turned into the lane.

Various evacuees came and went from our home. One lady with a little boy did a quick bunk when I went down with the measles. But it didn't help, as we heard later that her little boy had caught it anyway. Other airmen were billeted on us, including a pianist who used to thump away practising on our old piano. This airman would empty his chamber pot out of his bedroom window, which Mother did not go a lot on. Thank goodness the Vicar didn't choose one of those moments to call, with Father's duties to carry out during the week. Mother was too reserved to tell the airman to stop this practice; when we heard his window go up, we used to hope no one was walking by at the time.

My sister went to a show in London years later when she was an adult, and the pianist in the pit caught her attention – she seemed to recognise the wavy hair. On checking the names in the programme, sure enough, it was our chamber pot emptier.

Two nurses lived in the house next door when I was little. I can remember dear Nurse Whitlock, who was a jovial person. One day when our grandmother was staying with us, she noticed smoke coming from the front room of the nurses' home. The other nurse had been trying to light the fire, and had gone off to post a letter, forgetting that she had left a newspaper sheet against the grate to draw up the fire. Luckily Nurse Whitlock was in the back kitchen when Mother ran round to give the alarm. They had a small pond by the kitchen door, so Nurse scooped out buckets of water from the pond to put out the fire, which had burnt the whole corner of the room. It was only later that poor Nurse Whitlock noticed that some of her goldfish were missing. They had been sacrificed in saving the house. After Nurse Whitlock went to live in Warfield, her place was taken by Nurse Robinson, who became our neighbour through most of our childhood. Little were we to know that she was to deliver our own offspring when we were grown up and married. It was nice having an old friend helping us through childbirth.

As the war years progressed, so our little circle of childhood friends grew with the influx of evacuees. Some of these children were placed in the large houses around Bracknell. Even the well-off people had to play their part in opening their doors to accommodate the evacuees. I remember playing with a girl called Pauline who was staying in a large house with a croquet lawn in the back garden. I was never very good at croquet, and haven't had the chance to improve my game since. My sister used to play with a friend called Ivy Morrison, who was placed in a large house in Wick Hill; only three of these houses are left standing now. The other lovely houses are now just a memory. Jean thought it was very grand, as they were given tea by the maid in the kitchen. A maid dressed in black, complete with a white cap and frilly apron, also served tea to the children at a house in Church Road where Jean used to go and play.

I never received this star treatment in the houses that my friends were in, but if I did go into one of these large houses, I felt really out of my depth anyway. I found the atmosphere in these silent homes so formal and starchy that while playing there, I felt we had to speak in

The Bracknell Fire Brigade included women members in the war

just whispers to one another. If my friend disappeared to go up to her bedroom for something, I would sit there not moving while the sound of ticking from the large old clocks was the only thing breaking the silence. I was always glad when my friend came back down again, and also glad to get back home to our noisy house full of laughter and companionship with our airmen and Dutch boys etc.

Soon it was Cynthia's turn to arrive into our midst. Her stay with us was the longest of our evacuees, so she became almost like a sister to us. By this time we were all sleeping back in our bedroom again, and our three beds were all in a row, with Cynthia's in the middle. We even spent Christmas together, opening our stockings at dawn – none of us heard Father creep in with them during the night. Our parents made sure that Cynthia had her stocking to open too. It was one of our happiest Christmasses.

Our eldest sister expected to be called up for the services during this period, so she joined the local GTC while waiting. Mrs Booth, Miss Watson and Miss Strawson were three of the ladies in charge of the Girls Training Corp, which used to assemble at Ranelagh School for their training sessions. The local Home Guard also used Ranelagh School for training.

Cynthia was a pretty girl with lovely long hair which tended to curl, so unlike our own straight short hair, which was always cut by our local barber Mr Flower, in his shop in the old High Street. When one went into the barber's, one always had to step carefully over Mr Flower's large old red setter dog Kim, who always insisted on sprawling right in the doorway. Kim was a bit of a celebrity in the

106

The local GTC girls pictured in Raneleigh playing field

High Street, and he was patted and fussed from dawn until dusk. When old Kim died, Mr Flower replaced him with other red setters down through the years, and they were all named Kim. Bracknell High Street wouldn't have been the same without a Kim strolling about.

Pam Brown was Mr and Mrs Flower's evacuee, and I loved to fondle the old dog on my visits to play with Pam. I remember Mrs Flower coming down to the recreation ground looking for Pam, when we went playing in the field instead of going straight home, and saying that Pam would not be allowed to listen to Enid Blyton's 'Five' adventure stories on *Children's Hour* if she did not go straight home from school. We all loved the Enid Blyton Stories.

Mrs Flower's old-fashioned telephone had me speechless when she handed it to me one day to speak to Pam's mother in London, which in those days seemed so far away. I had never used one before. Mr Flower's hairstyles were the same for boys and girls, so we had to suffer the old clippers up the back of our necks.

OUR BOYS IN BLUE

As rooks in their hundreds fly home to rest,
The evening sun settles slowly in the west.
As the golden rays give way to a deepening blue,
The last rooks call, to the dwindling few.

An air of silence descends all around,
In the gathering twilight, there seems not a sound.
Then a soft summer breeze starts to rustle the trees,
Resembling the sound of the humming bees.

The first star appears, high in the blue,
Silently twinkling, giving hope all anew.
As the last ray of sun falls out of sight,
Other stars shine, to herald the night.

The sweet scent of roses fills the air,
A peaceful world, without a care.
Out venture creatures of the night,
The owls and the bats, in silent flight.

Hedgehogs come busily, foraging forth,
Quite unaware of the sounds from the north.
In the gathering dusk, and all around,
Quietly at first, approaches the sound.

Over the rooftops, they wing on their way,
Always at night, never by day.
Louder and louder, nearer and nearer,
Dark ghostly shapes get clearer and clearer.

Fathers and sons, brothers and chums,
All off to face the enemy's guns.
We try and slumber, but how can we sleep,
Praying to God to safely keep.

Those brave young men, in their nightly task
Of keeping us from the Fuehrer's grasp.
Searchlights go sweeping, while we are all sleeping,
Awaiting the dawn, for our loved ones' return.

Bill and Charlie, the airmen billeted with the family, and the author's father

Stars now are fading, a new day's awakening,
Birds start their singing, and flowers their opening.
The sounds from the south come slowly a-winging,
Heavily, wearily, their crews they are bringing.

But where are the ones who seem to be missing,
Lost in a war, not of their making?
Lost to their loved ones at home who are waiting,
Patiently waiting, and waiting, AND WAITING.

109

AFTER THE WAR

The four years following the war were mixed years of getting back to normal. Local youngsters wed sweethearts after meeting during their wartime service together. Some evacuees stayed on here in Bracknell, especially the ones who had grown into teenagers during this period, preferring village life in the country away from the back streets of London. Some other local girls waited and waited for the return of lost loved ones, hoping against hope that the message in a war telegram of 'missing presumed dead' was a mistake after all. Gradually as weeks turned into months, and months into years, the sad realisation dawned on them that their loved ones weren't coming home.

Rationing was to be with us in various forms until the beginning of the 1950s. Long queues formed outside shops on different days, when

Alice North unveiling Crowthorne's War Memorial. Her two sons were among the fallen

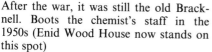

After the war, it was still the old Bracknell. Boots the chemist's staff in the
1950s (Enid Wood House now stands on
this spot)

Office girls clearing the snow in London
Road – 1950's

deliveries of certain foods were expected. Black marketing was rife, for
those who had the money. A friend asked if any cornflakes had been
delivered, and was told they had not. As she stood there a box of
groceries containing no less than six boxes of cornflakes were carried
out to a large limousine parked outside. Mum, queued for hours each
week when a Telford pie delivery was due. It was my job to queue
outside Mr Hollingsworth's shop, when an ice cream delivery came.
Queue jumpers were dealt with by being sent promptly to the back of
a queue; it was a policy of first come, first served.

Sweet rationing lasted quite a time, and one day I went with my
ration book to Mr Hollingsworth's and purchased a Mars bar with
my coupon, but on returning home, found that I had dropped it
somewhere along the way. As I ran back down Rochdale road, I
could see my weekly sweet ration lying on the path outside the
Church House, but before I could reach it, a lady came along pushing
a large heavy pram, and squashed it flat!

White parachute silk came in handy during this period, for making
silk underwear and baby clothes etc. Mum queued for hours one day,
just to get some curtain netting which looked like printed scrim, but
we thought it was wonderful as things were so scarce.

When one of my sisters left school, she went to work in the Food
Office in Archway House, Bracknell.

White weddings became more frequent after the war years, but
many girls had to make do with borrowed dresses, which were often

111

too short and a bad fit, but at least they were white, and gave a girl the chance to dress upon on her big day. As Dad was the verger, he used to let me know when a wedding was on, so I could go and wait by the wall. I must have watched dozens of weddings through my childhood.

School carried on much the same, but there was great excitement when we received four new tennis rackets, which had to be shared by the whole school.

To cheer us up after the war years, in 1945 the hottest April was recorded, when it was 82 degrees in the shade. The April sunshine brought May flowering tulips into bloom, and eastern counties growers were cutting asparagus. But this heatwave was followed on May Day Eve by a snowfall which lasted four and a half hours, with a nighttime temperature of 35 degrees. In the West Country, 12 degrees of frost damaged potatoes and strawberry crops. There was little damage to apples as the blossom had set, but in the Vale of Evesham soft fruit crops were the hardest hit.

When I reached the age of 14 in 1949, the school leaving age was put up to 15. A new classroom was built for these pupils in part of the buttercup field at the back of the school. That extra year spent in Mr Edward's class was to be one of the happiest of all my school years. I was quite sorry when the time approached for leaving. Our

Bullbrook Football Team

112

Old pupils ringing the school bell for the last time

football team won the cup, and we all went out into the playground for the presentation, expecting a large cup similar to the Fielden Cup. Imagine our disappointment when the cup turned out to be little bigger than an eggcup.

MARKET DAY

Going our way, on Market Day,
Not to delay, but our steps they would stray.
Drawn by the noise, as if in a greeting,
Hens were a-clucking, and lambs were a-bleating.

In through the gate, and there set before us,
Cows, pigs and sheep, all joined in the chorus.
Puppies and kittens, mind you're not smitten,
Probing small hands too often were bitten.

In to the pigs. Oh! What a pong,
Poor little lambs, bleating their song.
The cry of the calves, after their mothers,
But here in the bustle, nobody bothers.

There was still a farmyard for frolics – 1930's

114

The auctioneer's hammer comes down with a thud,
And the bull just sold is led off to stud.
Around to the cows, watch out for the muck!
Swishing wet tails, must remember to duck.

Big sorrowful eyes, as they stand and stare,
But try and escape, they would not dare.
Fluffy bright chicks, and stout walking sticks,.
Bikes, forks and prams, and frisky old rams,
All up for sale, along with the lambs.

The pub's overfilling, with farmers all swilling,
Onto the trains, the cattle are filling.
As slowly they ride off into the gloom,
For sadly tomorrow, it will be to their doom.

And the livestock market

115

The day's work all done, and everyone gone,
Dead chicks lie around, bright yellow on the ground.
The pens are all empty, devoid now of sound,
As a solitary feather is left floating around.

LEISURE ACTIVITIES

Bracknell Bowling Club's original clubhouse and green were situated in Rochdale Road, which leads from Church Road down past the original Baptist Church, fire station, the Labour Exchange building and the Church House and British Legion and out into the Old High Street.

The pretty bowling green had the church spire of Holy Trinity as a backcloth. Members included Mr Sarney, who was manager of Jacksons the gentlemen's outfitters, Mr Slyfield the timber merchant, Mr Thompson and his wife, the Rev. Anders, Mr Hatcher, who ran the library shop, Mr Vaughan, who worked at Hunton & Son and was the auctioneer for many years at Bracknell Market, and his wife. Mr and Mrs Payne and Miss Bessie Hollis, who ran a haberdashery shop with her sister for many years, and Mr and Mrs Wooding, who ran Gambriel's Greengrocers.

Next to the bowling green stood the Working Men's Club, which was later moved next to Bracknell College.

Bracknell at leisure. Members of Bracknell Bowling Club outside the original Rochdale Road clubhouse. This picture belongs to Marjory Buxton (on end of second row)

117

Joe Smith (far left, seated) organised outings to the sea. His daughter Rose (bottom right) still runs Smith's newsagents in Charles Square

For us children, the countryside was where we spent most of our spare time. But this could have some unusual consequences.

One day a girl came to school carrying a hedgehog, which promptly escaped and ran behind the large cupboard containing all of the school books. Mr Hill the caretaker was sent for, but the poor hedgehog could not be reached. It was left hoping it would come out later when the classroom was empty. But the poor thing had become wedged behind the cupboard and died. The smell became terrible, and all of the windows were opened, which didn't help. There was nothing for it, the huge cupboard had to be emptied of hundreds of books, and moved forward to retrieve the poor little offending hedgehog.

Mr Hill was a father figure loved by all of the children. he and Miss Swadling looked after all of the children's and teachers' needs for many years. Some of their jobs were not very nice ones.

In the early years at school, we used to go across to Bay Road to run our team races down the middle of the road. If a car should come along, the driver waited until the race was finished, and then proceed on his journey. In this day and age, one can't imagine a driver pulling up for a race to be finished, it would be all horn-blowing and rude gestures after two seconds.

While waiting for our turns to run, we sat looking for tiddlers in the brook, or picked some wild flowers from the water's edge.

Ascot Race Weeks would be so heavy with traffic passing the school, we were given that week off. Each year we looked forward to our picnics up at the racecourse. We always settled ourselves down near the Golden Gate, away from the crowds on the heath. The weather in those years always seemed to be sunny, as we sat waiting for the Royal Procession. For a few hours we were transported into another world. Finally the outriders would appear in their lovely red and gold tunics, the jingling of the polished brasses on the harnesses of the beautiful Windsor greys, and the creaking sounds of the lovely old carriages as they trundled over Ascot's bright green turf. The Royal Family were always smiling and waving, the ladies' complexions better than any film star's, hanging on to their pretty hats in the June breeze. After the procession had passed, we made our way up to the heath and stood opposite the Royal Box, which was always decorated with lovely bright blue hydrangeas. We didn't possess a pair of binoculars, so a friend with us passed me hers to look through at the Royal Family in the Royal Box. I had a job to focus them, when a man at my side said, 'I will show you, little girl,' as I handed him the binoculars. Our friend shouted at the man, 'Oh no you don't,' while at the same time grabbing her property out of his hands, whereupon he quickly melted back into the crowd again. The pickpockets and thieves had a field day at the crowded races.

One character who appeared each year was a tipster who called himself 'Prince Monolulu' or some similar-sounding name. This man was decked out in bright-coloured feathers and little else. With his face painted, he would strut about the heath shouting to all who were interested, 'I gottaa-a horse, I gottaa-a horse.' Ascot just wasn't the same without Prince Monolulu each year.

The public in those days could stand right up against the racecourse fence. Later the crowds on the heath were moved right back and penned off, and gypsies were not allowed on their old pitches. Some say that there was a gypsy curse on it afterwards, as each race week in years following was troubled with storms and heavy rain. One year a bolt of lightning struck a fence, and all of the punters leaning on it were struck down. Many were holding up umbrellas, which helped towards the tragedy. I believe that two people were killed, but it was several years ago now. In later years when I was older, I went to Ascot on my own, standing by the main entrance in the High Street, watching celebrities like Bebe Daniels and Ben Lyon, and Katie Boyle, who was Viscountess then. In the evenings we stood at the top

119

of Bracknell High Street, watching the large limousines carrying the lords and their ladies back home again.

Some of the rich splashed out on hiring lovely old restored stage-coaches for the journey to Ascot, and dressed the part in outfits of Georgian and Victorian times. It was a lovely sight to see, even if it was a shade uncomfortable for the passengers. It didn't take much imagination to picture olden times when these stagecoaches travelled the roads hereabout, only to be held up frequently by highwaymen.

The wonderful atmosphere of Ascot has changed through the years; there isn't the excitement of the old days, although it still attracts visitors from all over the world. The dastardly JR from *Dallas* was present a few years ago, and the colourful sight of Prince Monolulu's feathers have been replaced by Mrs Shilling's way-out hats, and Dame Edna wearing a model of the Sydney Opera House on her/his head! The procession no longer comes through the Golden Gates, as that part of the course was closed when the rebuilding of the new stands and clock tower commenced.

Bracknell was always busy on Ascot Race Weeks, and many local people went up to the course to earn a little extra spending money. For some housewives it was the highlight of the year. It was a friend's job to hold the starter's horse at the beginning of each race, back in the days when the starter rode a beautiful old horse down the course and raised the tapes manually.

It was strange to see large limousines parked in the High Street surrounded by a little circle of village men peering in at the dashboards, instead of the usual farm tractors, small cars or commercial vans of the locals. One just had to wait for the owners to emerge from the shop, dressed in all their finery for the race meeting. Often it was someone we would recognise from the newspaper gossip columns, and our curiosity satisfied, we continued our way to work, while they drove off in their large limousines to enjoy strawberry and cream teas, to see, and be seen, promenading at the races.

Back in our schooldays on our return after race week, the talk was all of what the Royalty wore each day. Snippets of information were passed around and pictures swapped for the scrapbooks.

After the war years, men were busy at work painting back in the road signs, also 'Bracknell' appeared once more over shop signs and commercial vehicles etc. It was time for Dad to remove all the large blackout shutters from the two halls. The gas masks were all called in, which was a pity, as they would have been quaint souvenirs by now. It was a lovely feeling to be free at last from these wartime precautions. But we still jumped when the siren sounded, before realising it was the all-clear sound now being used as a fire alert for the fire brigade.

The Young and Hopeful shows in the 1940s featured many talented young Bracknellians

121

As soon as it sounded, I and other local children would run to the fire station nearby in Rochdale Road to watch the firemen arrive, mostly on bicycles. Mr Harvey had a little van that screeched to a halt, and the bicycles were thrown down in all directions, and off they went, still struggling into their boots and tunics as the engine roared out of the station, their helmets thrown on their heads at jaunty angles in their haste for a quick turnout.

We were very proud of our firemen, as they had one of the fastest turnouts in the country. As the location of the fire was shouted to one another, some boys would jump on their bicycles and peddle off in hot pursuit to watch the excitement. Being girls, we were not allowed to do this, and had to be content with running home instead to tell our parents where the fire was that day. But very often a tell-tale pall of smoke appeared in the sky, and if it was a heath fire, the smoke would soon be smelt all over the village.

Sometimes these fires spread so rapidly that soon the sirens of Ascot and Crowthorne could be heard as more assistance was needed. In hot summers, it only needed a careless smoker, or a broken piece of glass in the undergrowth, to ignite one of these destructive

This band played at most of the local dances. In this picture, taken in the Victoria Hall, Sid Peters is on drums

122

fires. The smell would sometime hang over the village for days afterwards.

Bracknell during the 1940s, and 1950s had several excellent amateur dramatic societies, which held their plays in the Victoria Hall and the Church House. Of these the most memorable were the Bracknell Dramatic Society productions, and also the plays produced by a group who went under the name of the Bracknell Mummers. The seats were at the very reasonable prices of 6s at the front of the hall,

Doreen Mills was a soloist singer in local shows

123

which is 30p; 4s (20p) and 2s 6d (13p) at the back. But one has to remember that people's wages were much lower in those days. I was earning the princely sum of £2 a week in the 1950s, and men with families to keep were earning in the region of £6.

Quite a few famous people used to come to our local plays. There was a lot of excitement when Diana Dors arrived one night in her large limousine at the Victoria Hall, with her luxurious long platinum-blonde hair glistening in the evening lights.

There was another group of young people who called themselves the Young and Hopefuls. Their musical song and dance shows were eagerly looked forward to each year. Mr Ray Townsend was the

Davina Morris, who sang in the operatic society

lighting manager for the shows, and his magic lighting effects were good enough for the London Palladium.

The East Berkshire Operatic Society, whose chairman was Mr Hebbron and musical director Mr William Mitchell, produced *HMS Pinafore* etc. One of their leading ladies was Miss Davina Morris, who appeared in many of the operatic society productions. Sadly Davina died at the early age of 26, in the British Hospital in Buenos Aires,- after being taken ill aboard the RML *Arlanza*, on which she was working as a hairdresser. Her beautiful singing voice had already earned her bronze medals and certificates. Her memorial service was held in Holy Trinity, six weeks after her death.

TWO WELL-KNOWN WOMEN

NURSE ROBINSON was a district nurse for Bracknell right up until her retirement. At first she carried out her duties on a bicycle, and then learned to drive when a small car was provided for her work, which made the many miles she had to travel each day a lot easier. It seemed very strange at first having a car running up and down the lane, which was stony, and kicking up a dust in summer, but luckily Robbie didn't drive like the characters in *Miami Vice*.

Nurse Robinson's sister was a piano teacher in her house in London Road, now the Met Office car park. Another Bracknell piano teacher was the blind pianist Mr James, who lived in Church Road for many

'Nurse Robbie' was another well-known Bracknell figure

years, and Gladys Phillips was also a piano and elocution teacher in Lily Hill.

I was never able to master the keyboard very well, but my sister Jean was very good and played at socials. She even mastered the church organ under Mr Faulkner's guidance, and used to practise alone in the church of an evening as a young girl. That is, until a bat flew out of the rafters one night after dark and swooped around the organ light. She never practised at night again. One of our spinster teachers told us stories of bats catching in people's hair, which was stupid as it made us afraid of them, when in fact they are quite loveable little creatures.

ELSIE SUDDABY was born in Leeds in 1893. She was known as the Lass with the Delicate Air. Elsie's soprano voice was often heard on the radio at the height of her fame. She had a strong following with her concert appearances. Her soprano voice was often heard accompanying Kathleen Ferrier's contralto singing. There are many CDs available with these two lovely singers of the past together. Sadly Kathleen died of cancer at the age of 41. Elsie died in 1980 at the age of 87 years.

Although born in Leeds, Elsie moved to Bracknell from Hampstead at the start of the Second World War. Her stay in Bracknell was to last for 20 years. It probably would have been much longer if Elsie's home had not been compulsory purchased to make way for Bracknell New Town.

The haven Elsie found to live with her friend Miss Allen, away from the worst of

Elsie Suddaby, the Leeds-born professional singer who moved to Bracknell

the London Blitz, could not escape the attentions of the bulldozers, and her home at Stanley Villas in Church Road was destroyed along with the rest of old Bracknell. But there are still people in Bracknell who remember this gentle lady with a beautiful voice. As a child, I have a faint recollection of Elsie singing the *Messiah* in Holy Trinity, but I was too young to be allowed to sit through this long concert. I wonder if anyone else remembers this concert?

THE BULLDOZERS ARRIVE

Through the sad sixties, Bracknell began to resemble one of Hitler's bombing sites. Our thriving little market town was being systematically destroyed street by street. Winston's words 'We shall fight them street by street' were remembered, but this was a fight we could not win, and Bracknellians had to stand by and watch as the rape of their town began.

We three sisters had married in the years 1954–6. After having our names on the council housing list, our only hope of being housed seemed to be if we had several babies in a row, as each child meant extra points. But none of us wanted this type of start to married life. When my sister's fiancé was being sent to Korea for two years, they decided to get married before he left, hoping that in the next two years they would be further up the housing list. My eldest sister married the next year, after a friend offered them a flat in Church Road, so she was lucky indeed.

Our brother-in-law came home from Korea, still being no further up the housing list, and I got married in the April of 1956, so poor Mum and Dad had two newly married couples living with them. Dear old Ferndale resembled the war years once again with every inch of space being used.

Later, an office friend told us some rooms for rent under theirs were becoming vacant, so we moved to Winkfield for six years. Other local girls had to live in caravans for years, out in Warfield Park etc.

After six years in Winkfield and two children later, we were at last given the chance to move back into our home town, but only because of the kindness of our old neighbours, who were leaving the district. It was a lovely feeling to be following the furniture van back to Bracknell and home once more.

I was very glad to be leaving Winkfield, as we suffered constantly from the Berkshire Belly tummy bug, but on our return to Bracknell we still suffered, along with everyone else. After decorating the house throughout to our liking, the winter of 1963 was one of the coldest on record, and we found that the roof had let in the snow during one of the worst blizzards, so we had to spend hours in the loft, taking out buckets of snow to save the ceilings coming down.

The next bombshell came with a Compulsory Purchase Order dropping through the letter box. All of us had to move: my parents in

129

181

NEW TOWNS ACT, 1965.
BRACKNELL DEVELOPMENT CORPORATION.
COMPULSORY PURCHASE ORDER NUMBER 28, 1963.

N O T I C E   OF   E N T R Y.

TO: Mr. J.P. Briggs

OF: Cotheridge, Rochdale Road, Bracknell.

WHEREAS by virtue of an Order made by the Minister of Housing and
Local Government on the Twelfth day of July One thousand nine hundred and
sixty five confirming with modification the Bracknell Development Corporation
Compulsory Purchase Order Number 28, 1963 made by the Bracknell Development
Corporation (hereinafter called "the Corporation") under the New Towns Act, 1946,
the Corporation are authorised to purchase compulsorily the land described in
the Schedule hereto

AND WHEREAS on the Fifth day of September One thousand nine hundred and sixty
five the New Towns Act, 1965 came into effect

AND WHEREAS Notice to Treat for the said property has been served upon you
and every owner of the land

N O W   THEREFORE the Corporation in exercise of the power conferred upon them
by the New Towns Act, 1965, hereby give you notice that they will on or after
the   **Thirty first**   day of   **July**   One thousand nine
hundred and **sixty seven** enter on and take possession of the land described in
the Schedule hereto

THE SCHEDULE BEFORE REFERRED TO

Number on Map.	Ordnance Survey (Edition of 1932) Map 1/2500 Sheets Berkshire XXXIX-9, XXXIX-13, XXXIX-14, and Parcel Nos.	Quantity, Description and Situation of Lands and Buildings.
59	Part 804 formerly in Parish of Warfield	0.104 acre or thereabouts comprising dwellinghouse, garage, garden and premises known as Cotheridge, Rochdale Road, Bracknell.

Dated this   14th   day of   July   1967

J.V.ROWLEY
General Manager and duly authorised Officer.

Farley Hall,
Binfield,
Bracknell. Berks.

130

Nurse Whitlock, who served the community for 35 years

Victoria Road, my sister in Station Road, my mother-in-law in Ralphs Ride, and ourselves in Rochdale Road.

The next four years were to be one upset after another. Pumps were left going all night so that residents couldn't sleep, and Brown's yard burnt down, nearly taking our parents house which was next door, with it. It was like trying to live on a bomb-site. Windows had to be kept closed as the dust of buildings being knocked down covered everywhere with red dust.

Hedgehogs and other wild creatures had to be rescued from the deep trenches they had fallen into the night before. The chopped-up remains of wildlife were to be seen everywhere: toads, frogs, slow-worms and hedgehogs weren't quick enough to escape the jaws of the bulldozers. Birds sat forlornly watching as their nesting sights were destroyed.

Then came our turn for a visit from the Corporation man. After quickly looking over our property, the time came to discuss our needs. He had the annoying habit of continually jingling his keys and money in his pocket. With each visit this jingling got on my nerves, as if he were in haste to get off to the next householder, and not once did he sit down to discuss the situation we were in, but stood, continually jingling and jangling. Because we liked a nice home, he announced that we must live with paintbrushes in our hands. He couldn't have read our notes beforehand, as he would have seen that my husband was a self-employed decorator.

131

Nurse Ruth Heathman was one of the last nurses to stay in the Victoria Road nurses' home, demolished to make way for a car park in 1966

But life always has a funny side. A gigantic hole had been dug where the tailor's shop used to be in Church Road. At dusk one night, John noticed a hedgehog crawling around in the bottom, so he came in for a ladder to go down and get it. The ladder wasn't long enough, so our longest extending ladder was fetched. This was only just long enough to reach the bottom. Hubby climbed down, but hadn't thought how to pick the prickly creature up. By now it was almost dark as John ran back for gloves and bucket and scrambled down the muddy hole just to rescue one frightened hedgehog.

After Mother had moved, in her haste she had left a mirror behind in the kitchen which she wished to have in her new house. Once our homes were handed over to the demolition gangs, one felt like a trespasser going back for little keepsakes. So I quickly went through our garden gate, which joined our two properties at the back. I had great difficulty trying to climb up and squeeze through the small

132

kitchen window and landed in the sink rather unceremoniously. After rescuing the mirror, something made me try the door, which opened and I walked quickly out! What a performance! it was open all of the time, and there was I squeezing through the small window.

It wasn't pleasant having to live for four years in a landscape of mounting heaps of rubble all around us, and there was I still keeping the garden pretty, while the desolation crept up to our boundaries. A futile task, on reflection.

It was during this time while cutting the front hedge that the world suddenly started to spin around me, and I found myself crawling on hands and knees, with shears in hands, trying to find the front door. I was to spend the next four weeks lying in a darkened room, suffering from Ménière's disease. When I tried to look out of my bedroom window, I saw two church spires, not one. This disease stayed with me on and off for four years, and during the periods of illness resting in bed, the noise of bulldozers all day and water pumps on all night didn't help. One day, feeling better, I was standing washing up at my kitchen sink, by the open window, when two large chunks of cement fell into my washing-up water. It was the last straw! The demolition gangs had started to pull down the adjoining property, while we were still living in ours. My one and only letter was sent off to the Development Corporation that day. How could our children play in our garden with chunks of concrete falling everywhere. The harassment next door was halted temporarily, after my letter.

While I was busy doing my washing one day, a member of the demolition gang asked if he could show the man standing on the doorstep with him our lemon bathroom suite, as he was selling it to him. They couldn't even wait until after we had settled elsewhere. Old people were less able to put up with the harassment of having to move, and many died broken-hearted during this period.

When the Church House was demolished, many happy memories went with it. This hall was very popular for wedding receptions, dances and socials. Local clubs put on stage plays and concerts. During the war the hall was used as a clearing station for evacuees, who often had to sleep on the floor overnight while waiting for local billets to be found. Later it was taken over by the Air Ministry for RAF purposes. Many ENSA concerts and dances were held there, and the occasional conference. The floorboards were left in a very poor state by the RAF, as they were in many old mansions which were taken over in the war, so dances were no longer held there. The Victoria Hall was then used for the local firemens balls etc.

MODERN BRACKNELL

Bracknell's prosperity continued to grow through the 1970s and 1980s, but unfortunately alongside this prosperity has also grown the violence. Is it to become a town where none of the inhabitants feel safe any more, even in their own homes? I hope not.

We all need space to breathe and find recreation, but if modern developers get their way, the urban sprawl will stretch to London eastwards and Reading westwards, with every little patch of green countryside gobbled up in between.

The little wildlife that we have left will disappear, Bracknell will not be a place for badgers, foxes or amphibians. The suggestion that Skimped Hill be used as a garden park area for the population was laughed at. But why? Other large towns have central gardens for relaxation during snatched lunch hours. Who wants to sit on the seats in Bracknell's town centre, where the tall buildings cause such a down draught that dust, litter and dangerous heavy billboards are swirled all around.

Battling Joe Brant, who campaigned for the disabled and blind community

Dear Joe Brant did his best for the disabled and blind community in getting rid of these obstacles in the town centre, but now that Joe has gone, they are appearing in ever increasing numbers. On a windy day, these heavy boards are lifted up and thrown several yards along the High Street. It is only a matter of time before a small child is badly injured.

Joe might not have gone about things in the correct way, but his efforts and ideas were always good and sound ones for the well-being of the inhabitants of Bracknell.

Now Joe has gone, and rest his case,
Who will step in and take his place?
Battl'ing Joe became his name,
Without him, Bracknell's not the same.

Who will now speak for the little man?
Fighting for justice to be done.
In Warfield, and in Binfield too,
Let them not meet their Waterloo.

Let there be space, for trees and sky,
Not concrete jungle, where birds can't fly.
Duck ponds and park, in a nearby place,
Where amphibians can live, alongside the human race.

Must it become a desert land
Of spreading concrete, at every turn?
Developers now please, give our area a miss,
Must the whole of Bracknell now look like this?

(Now vandals are joining developers in disfiguring Bracknell)

CHANGING TIMES

Changing scenes, and a changing lifestyle since our grandparent's time, when Alice, my grandmother, after a long hard day's work down in the kitchen of General Buller's house, sat up in her tiny attic bedroom watching the arrival of the gentry in their carriages up the long drive to the house. She and the other maids would marvel at the elaborate silk dresses worn by the ladies. Not for them the hours of recreation that young people enjoy now in the 1990s. If a young girl became pregnant in olden times, she was tin-canned out of a village in disgrace. One has to wonder what happened to those poor girls afterwards. Anyone who misbehaved received a dose of rough music. A tin-canning took place in 1874, in protest of the 2nd Lord Ormathwaite, who was rumoured to be ill-treating his wife Lady Emily, who was highly thought of by the villagers of Warfield. By October the people decided they could not remain silent any longer, and 400-strong rabble marched up to the Ormathwaite mansion banging drums, saucepans and pails, creating such a disturbance that years later this ghostly rabble has been heard on many occasions, marching up to the now non-existent Warfield Park House.

My grandmother Alice died in 1940, so was spared the trauma of seeing another World War. Life for us changed dramatically after the war, with modern architects building masses of office blocks all looking like piles of matchboxes. The steep tunnels dug out like rabbit warrens were so obviously designed by men who have never had to push youngsters in pushchairs to reach the town centre.

The office blocks, although ugly, give greater comfort than our office back in the 1950s. After cycling from Winkfield through the snow, my friend Audrey and I arrived not to a warm office, but to one filled with smoke, as the older boiler had only just been lit prior to our arrival at 8.30 a.m. Every door and window had to be thrown open to let out the smoke, which in turn let in the winter's frosty blast. We sat in overcoats and gloves almost until lunchtime each day.

One day we arrived to find the office flooded, so had to sit with our feet up on the foot rests out of the water, with our chairs stood in several inches of water. Our boss rang head office to explain the situation, but we weren't given the day off, only told to make sure the electric leads to the adding machines were up out of the water. In spite of the hardships, they were a grand bunch of girls, and we had

137

many happy times. On market days we often had to dodge straying animals on our way back to the office after our lunch breaks. One day Jeanette came flying through the door at great speed, slamming it shut behind her, just as a great thud was heard from the other side of the closed door. An escaped billy goat had chased her all down the London Road, and the farmers, unable to help her, were shouting 'Run gal run!'

Changing times and changing scenes. Whereas other towns have lovingly restored their old buildings, here in Bracknell they have been systematically destroyed bit by bit. Sadly the words of Ian Yarrow, that there is little of beauty to be seen, have been made to come true. Beauty was here, but now is just a memory.

BIBLIOGRAPHY

Broome F.W. (Rev.), *1851 Bracknell*. 1951.

Canning, J., *Fifty Great Ghost Stories*, 1984.

Harris, J. and Stanton G., *A History of Winkfield*.

Long B. (Rev.), *An Historical Sketch of Wokingham*. 1930.

Shoreland E., *The Pish (Parish) of Warfield & Easthampstead*. 1967.

Prescott, M. Crow, *On the Thorne*.

Smart, P., *Extracts from The Past Ascot*. 1985.

Timbrell, R.J.C., *Chavey Up Down and Around*. 1983.

Wokingham Society. President Cross A, Wokingham, A, *A Chronology*. 1978.

History of Britain, Consultant Editor Professor Emeritus W.G.V. Balchin

Ellmann, R. *Oscar Wilde*.

Encyclopedia Britannica.

Yarrow, I., *Berkshire*. 1952.